Tangible Realities

By
Cecelia Frances Page

iUniverse, Inc.
New York   Bloomington

Tangible Realities

iUniverse books may be ordered through booksellers or by contacting:

iUniverse
1663 Liberty Drive
Bloomington, IN 47403
www.iuniverse.com
1-800-Authors (1-800-288-4677)

ISBN: 978-1-4401-1459-5 (sc)
ISBN: 978-1-4401-1460-1 (ebk)

Printed in the United States of America

iUniverse rev. date: 1/05/2009

Contents

PREFACE

TANGIBLE REALITIES is a dynamic book to read. There are many tangible realities that affect our daily lives. It is worth seeking truth, wisdom and tangible knowledge in the world.

There are sixty, worthwhile topics presented in this book. Social issues are included such as Jenny, A Very Inclined Person, Melissa's Experience As An Airline Hostess, Village Life, Intellectual People, Ambitious People, Laura's New Job, Domesticated People, The Exceptional Teacher and Talk Shows.

Creative topics are Creative Introspections, Useful Inventions, Pottery Making, Gourmet Cooks, Famous Artists, Film Making, Sketchings and Doll Makers. Political topics are Peace Corps Service, World Crises, Political Challenges, Important Presidents of the United States of America, Wall Street Crisis, Democrats Versus Republicans, Delegates At The United Nations, Presidential Debates In 2008, Television Broadcast By News Reporters, Coping With Changes and Truthful Statements.

Adventure topics are Surfboard Performers, Unusual Episodes, Oceanside Adventures, Novelties, The Country Hay Ride, Italian Escapades, Cheryl's Hitch Hiking Experiences and Flight to Paradise.

Science fiction topics are UFO Observations and Telos, The Underground Domain.

Religious topics are Master Hilarion's Teachings, Mary Magdalene Mystery, Karmic Situations, Metaphysical Books and Peaceful Moments. Health topics are Respiratory Problems and How To Sleep Well. Other miscellaneous topics are The Vacuum, Books and More Books, Magazine Memories, Musical Instrument Tuners, Japanese Gardens, The Pub, Proficient Linguists, Bull Fighters, Rome and Juliet, Shakespeare Personified, Family Pho Housekeepers and Maids, Facing Up To Chall Secretaries Make A Difference, Inalienable R Coping With Changes and Truthful Stateme

ABOUT THE AUTHOR

Cecelia Frances Page has published five, original screenplays and three, original, poetry books. The original screenplays are entitled <u>Walking in the Light</u>, <u>Flashbacks</u>, <u>Celestial Connections I and II</u> and <u>Adventures in Lemuria I and II</u>. The three, original, poetry books are entitled <u>Cosmic Dimensions</u>, <u>Vivid Impressions</u> and <u>Significant Introspections</u>. Cecelia Frances Page has written over five hundred, original poems. Several of her poems are published in <u>The World's Best Poems of 2004 and 2005</u>.

Cecelia has been writing since the age of 19. She has written 38 books. Some of her books published by iUniverse are entitled: <u>Westward Pursuit</u>, <u>Opportune Times</u>, <u>Imagine If...</u>, <u>Fortunately</u>, <u>Mystical Realities</u>, <u>Magnificent Celestial Journeys</u>, <u>Extraordinary Encounters</u>, <u>Brilliant Candor</u>, <u>Expand Your Awareness</u>, <u>Seek Enlightenment Within</u>, <u>Vivid Memories of Halcyon</u>, <u>Awaken to Spiritual Illumination</u>, <u>Adventures on Ancient Continents</u>, <u>Pathways to Spiritual Realization</u>, <u>Celestial Connections</u>,

Phenomenal Experiences, Celestial Beings from Outer Space, Awesome Episodes, Incredible Times, Interpretations of Life, New Perspectives, Tremendous Moments, Amazing Stories and Articles, Horizons Beyond, Fascinating Topics, Certain People Make A Difference, Tremendous Moments, Amazing Stories and Articles, Power of Creative and Worthwhile Living, Tangible Realities and more.

Cecelia Frances Page has a B.A. and M.A. in Education with a focus in English, Speech and Psychology. Cecelia is an excellent pianist. She is a piano and voice teacher, author, educator, philosopher, photographer and artist. Cecelia believes that creative abilities and talents can be achieved. Cecelia Frances Page continues to write more, worthwhile books to inspire her readers.

ONE

JENNY, A VERY INCLINED PERSON

Very inclined people have a particular disposition or bent of mind. They have certain likings and preferences. We all have tendencies to like certain interests, certain hobbies and we all pursue certain ambitions.

Jenny Granger was an ambitious person. She had many hobbies and interests. Jenny had strong opinions and beliefs about politics and religion. She was raised as a Christian. She was a democrat.

Jenny was 27 years old. She was a registered voter. She believed in the Democratic Party. Jenny believed in social and health programs for the impoverished people and senior citizens in America. Democrats focus on the needs of the middle and lower class.

Jenny strongly believed in the promotion of Social Security, Social Service Programs, Medicare and Medical Programs to help people in need. Approximately 95% of the people in America are in the middle class and lower class. Many of these people need financial protection. Without government programs this majority of the American people would be in financial difficulties. Jenny believed in the protection of the American people.

Jenny was a staunch believer in and promoter of healthcare programs. She believed in reasonable co-payment plans. Healthcare recipients should not have to pay more than 20% of the cost of pharmacy medications and doctors' bills. Hospital and surgery bills should be covered within insurance plans.

Religious beliefs and principles were important to Jenny Granger. She attended the Unitarian Church. Unitarians believe in world unity and peace in America and the world. They believe in the Ten Commandments in the Bible. "Love thy neighbor as thyself."

Jenny had grown up as a Unitarian. Because of the liberal beliefs and social concepts established in the Unitarian Church she has developed a broader, more open awareness about religious values and truths. Jenny was a thinker and doer. She wanted to enlighten others with her more inclined viewpoints and awareness.

Jenny was an active member in The League of Women Voters and Mothers of Peace. She believed in protecting the environment and natural resources. Jenny supported environmental programs such as the Sierra Club, 4-H Club, The Grange, Environmental Studies, Girl Scouts and Boy Scouts.

Because Jenny was very inclined to state her opinions and beliefs she was able to influence her family, friends and acquaintances. She participated in V.I.P. which means Vegetarian Inclined People. She was a vegan because she did not believe in animals being killed for meat. She did not eat meat or dairy products.

During the presidential election in 2004 Jenny took a strong stand about political issues. She strongly believed in civil rights, equal pay in jobs, cutting taxes, improving education and increasing health benefits and improving health programs.

Jenny believed in the dignity and well being of humanity. She was a humanitarian. She believed in justice, prosperity and happiness for everyone. Yes, Jenny was a self directed, strong willed person. She worked on an environmental studies program in her region. She had specific ideas of how to help to improve farm lands, water resources and living conditions for hundreds of miles around her region. Jenny was a helpful, resourceful person. She was of true service to many people.

TWO

MELISSA'S EXPERIENCE AS
A FLIGHT ATTENDANT

Flight attendants have the responsibility to make passengers feel comfortable and safe. They escort passengers to their seats and they help to serve snacks, drinks and meals during the flight.

Flight attendants must check passengers to be sure their luggage is secured in the overhead lockers or under their seats. The luggage must be properly secured with the locker closed so that luggage does not fall down or slide from under the seat into the isles. Loose luggage can be dangerous. Passengers could be injured from falling luggage.

If passengers are injured then the airline could be held accountable. The airline could be sued for negligence or lack of safety. So attendants must ensure that all passengers are safe.

Melissa Gregory decided to become a flight attendant. She had graduated from high school in June. She enrolled in a six months' flight attendant training program. Melissa was required to weigh no more than 120 pounds. She was expected to be healthy and tidy. She also must be on time whatever work schedule she was assigned to.

Melissa attended daily classes to prepare to become an airline hostess. She learned the duties and responsibilities of a flight attendant. She was given an attendant's uniform. The uniform was navy blue, with a white, long sleeved blouse, a navy blue jacket and matching pants.

The airline uniform was attractive on Melissa. She was 5 feet, 5 inches tall. She looked well groomed and professional. She wore a flower on her jacket. Her hair was blonde and her eyes were clear blue. She had curly hair which was styled in a modern fashion. Melissa had a beautiful face.

Once Melissa completed her flight attendant training course she was ready to begin working. She worked for Paradise Airlines. She had a cheerful disposition. She smiled at the passengers as she served them snacks and meals. She was attentive about serving them whatever they requested such as chosen cold, soft drinks, coffee or tea. She was careful to ensure that each passenger received their requested meal. Passengers could choose one out of two possible choices during lunch and at dinner time.

Melissa got along with the pilots and other flight attendant. She started on a work schedule from 7 a.m. until 7 a.m. the next morning. She was on the airplane over night. The next day she had time off from 7a.m. until 7 p.m. Then she started work at 7 p.m. that night and worked until 7 a.m. the next morning. Melissa followed an irregular, work schedule.

Melissa enjoyed her job as a flight attendant. She encountered sick people on flights. Some passengers had air sickness because oxygen content was thinned out high up in the sky. Some people had colds, flu and stomach aches. Melissa brought aspirin or Tylenol to passengers in pain. Oxygen masks were put over the nose and mouths of passengers who were suffering from lack of sufficient oxygen.

Melissa worked for eight months without any serious dangers. During air flights wind currents caused the airplane to jerk and waver. Yet the airplane continued on its flight to its destination. The air flights were regular and passengers made it to their expected destinations.

One day after Melissa began working on her next flight she continued to do her regular duties. She was busy serving the passengers. The airplane flew high in the sky for several hours. It was dark and the wind began to blow very fiercely. Melissa looked out of several windows in the airplane. She saw fires blazing at the propellers on the left wing.

Melissa rushed to tell the pilots about the fire. They already knew about the fire. They had to turn off the left propeller. Melissa was worried about what would happen next. She wondered whether the airplane might burn up. The pilot told Melissa to go to warn the other flight attendants to prepare for an emergency landing.

The airplane was flying over the ocean. There were 200 passengers, 2 pilots and 4 flight attendants on the plane. Everyone was in danger. Melissa tried to remain calm.

The passengers were sleeping in their airline seats. Some passengers had on earphones and were listening to music. Others were reading magazines and books. The pilot announced over the intercom that the airplane was on fire. He told passengers to prepare for an emergency landing in the ocean.

Melissa walked around to calm passengers and to assist them in putting on their life jackets. Rubber rafts were stored in the lower section of the airplane. Once the airplane landed in the ocean the rubber rafts would be released into the ocean. The passengers would have to exit out of the emergency doors and swim to the rafts.

Many passengers were upset and began to panic as the plane dived down into the ocean. They had their life jackets on. The emergency doors were quickly opened. The passenger got up and rushed to the nearest, exit doors. They jumped out of the plane and swam towards the closest rafts. They crawled on to the rafts.

Two hundred passengers plus the pilots and four flight attendants managed to get onto rafts. There were 21 rafts. 10 passengers got onto each raft. The flight attendants went to different rafts to assist the passengers. The passengers were frightened but relieved to be still alive.

Melissa was in one raft with ten passengers. She tried to calm them down. She said, "Don't panic! Don't rock the raft! Try to remain calm! There are bottles of water and some packed food for emergencies stored in sealed packets on this raft. When you get thirsty and hungry you may open a sealed packet and help yourselves to what you need."

The rubber rafts full of people drifted in the ocean. Meanwhile the airplane sank deep into the ocean and disappeared. Hours went by as the 21 rubber rafts drifted in the ocean. The stars in the sky twinkled. Melissa looked up at the moon and stars in the night sky. She tried to remain calm.

Passengers took out food from the sealed areas. There were crackers, pudding in cups and water. They ate some of the emergency food. Finally they tried to rest and go to sleep. The rafts bobbed up and down in the ocean. It was getting colder and colder.

Passengers and crew were shivering in the cold night air. It became windy. Some passengers were cold and wet without hats and jackets. They were very uncomfortable because they were so cold. Fortunately there were blankets in the sealed areas. Melissa and other flight attendants on other rafts told the passengers to help themselves to blankets and wrap themselves up in dry blankets. As a result they were warmer.

The next day the sun came up from the east. The day began to warm up. The passengers and crew were able to become warmer and dryer. They ate more stored food and sipped some water. However, they were worried about what was going to happen to them. The sun became hotter and more piercing. Ocean currents moved swiftly across the ocean.

The passengers were restless and worried how long it would be before they were rescued. They were sitting close together in the rafts. There were children and toddlers in some rafts and several babies were among the passengers. The babies needed special care. They had to be fed with milk and needed their diapers changed regularly to be comfortable.

The odor of smelly diapers was unpleasant. The mothers had brought some fresh diapers with them. The five babies needed attention and they cried when they needed attention. Other passengers were disturbed by the babies crying.

The ocean currents became swifter. Waves were beginning to break over the rafts and people were getting wet and uncomfortable from the ocean waves. Everyone had to endure the ocean waves.

Melissa decided to sing some folk songs. She asked everyone to sing along with her. They were getting wet and uncomfortable. She hoped that singing along would strengthen the passengers' determination to survive in her raft. She began singing O Susanna. The passengers decided to sing along with Melissa. Other people on other rafts joined in and began singing O Susanna as well.

Melissa sang The Red River Valley next. The people on all the rafts joined in and sang The Red River Valley. Then Melissa sang The Sound of Music. Everyone joined in and sang The Sound of Music.

The passengers became less restless. The singing united them and they were more relaxed. The airplane's captain spoke to everyone. He said, "I sent messages about the airplane's disastrous fire before leaving the plane and gave our exact location. We should soon see rescue squads searching for us and coming to pick us up. Have faith and be patient. Help is on the way. Shout as soon as you see airplanes searching for us."

Within another six hours rescue planes flew over the rafts. The passengers were relieved and grateful to see airplanes circling above them. Soon helicopters summoned by the search planes arrived equipped with chairs secured on the end of two, thick ropes. The chairs were lowered from 8 helicopters hovering over the rafts and passengers held the chairs steady while women and children clambered in the chairs first.

One by one the passengers were picked up and seated in the helicopters which took them back to the mainland and kept returning until finally all the passengers and crew were safe again. Melissa felt much better. She knew she had helped to save passengers' lives on that flight.

THREE

CREATIVE INTROSPECTION

Creative introspection is a process of using one's imagination and creative ingenuity to achieve worthwhile endeavors. Creative individuals are inventors, composers, writers, innovative cooks, original painters, artists, sculptors and researchers.

The intuitive awareness of creative people helps them to experience creative thoughts. They are capable of thinking of ideas beyond their time. Such individuals change the world with their creativity.

Benjamin Franklin was a creative person with insight and introspective ideas. He invented kites which had metal conductors attached to them. Franklin discovered electricity. Nichola Tesla discovered alternating currents in electricity. He continued to create a car which could run on hydrogen separated from the oxygen elements in water. The hydrogen fuel was clean and did not pollute the Earth's atmosphere. He developed high voltage towers to conduct electricity. He also developed a model and drawings of spaceships. His creative ideas for the invention of hydro engines which would run on water led to a very worthwhile invention.

Leonardo Da Vinci, who lived in the late 15th and early 16th centuries was a very creative person. His thoughts were beyond his time. He created models of aircraft and advanced ships. He was an artist and was known for painting The Last Supper with Jesus Christ and his twelve disciples.

Leonardo Da Vinci drew drawings of a man with 4 arms and legs. This was a three dimensional man representing the ideal proportions of the human figure. Leonardo Da Vinci drew airplanes. No one had drawn aircraft before this, centuries before aircraft were invented.

Pythagoras, who lived many centuries before Jesus Christ, was a mathematician. He had a school in ancient Greece and taught many advanced, geometry theorems including his famous right-angle triangle theorem: the square on the hypotenuse equals the sum of the squares on the other two sides. He also taught many of the important, geometry theorems discovered by the ancient Egyptians many years before he was born. Many of these ancient theorems are still taught by monks in some English Public Schools, including Radcliffe College a near neighbor of Sir Isaac Newton's School in Melton, Mowbray, Leicestershire. Pythagoras taught many advanced theorems and his students solved many number theory problems under his guidance. He was also a philosopher. He lived to be 100 years of age. He was quite advanced for his time.

William Shakespeare was progressive for his time. He was born in Stratford-upon-Avon in Warwickshire, England. He was part owner of the Globe Theatre in London, England which was built in 1599. His theatrical company was called the Lord Chamberlain's Men. The house where he lived with his wife is still open for visitors, and also the pub where he drank beer is still there near the River Avon and is open daily. It is well worth a visit as William Shakespeare's plays are still performed daily by first class Shakespearian actors and actresses. Many are so good that they often use their experience in William Shakespeare's plays to embark on a career in Hollywood films.

William Shakespeare wrote many stage plays about historical, political and social events, He used elegant English language in his dialogue. His characters responded to social issues. Their dialogue was quite poetic. Shakespeare wrote tragedies and comedies. He wrote over fifty plays and sometimes performed on the stage at the Royal Shakespeare Theatre built beside the beautiful, peaceful River Avon with the royal swans completing the quiet scene. His wife's home, known as Ann Hathaway's Cottage is still open for visitors and tourists to visit in Stratford-upon-Avon.

Shakespeare's plays were written down and eventually published in England by friends and associates. His plays have become well known and famous in the western world. He is known as one of the greatest writers in the world. He was a creative person who used introspection.

Creative, more advanced individuals change the world with their ideas, talents and creative abilities. They are introspective and innovative because they awaken and communicate with their creativity. We are fortunate to benefit from creative people.

FOUR

VILLAGE LIFE

Village life is special and worthwhile. Villagers become well acquainted on a frequent basis. They become like aunts, uncles, brothers and sisters. The daily gossip is communicated when villagers gather together in local stores, saloons and restaurants.

When villagers go to get their mail every day, they visit inside and outside the store on long, porch seats. They gather together at swimming holes to go swimming. Most villagers are friendly and sociable. They know each other well because they participate in village activities.

Villagers generally attend church together. They go to potlucks, birthday parties and school functions.

Neighbors know each other for many years. They help each other through hard times and dangerous experiences. Villagers bond together during social occasions and challenging moments.

The Williams lived in Lakeview, California. They had limited water in Oroville. The villagers had to conserve their water supply so that their neighbors would have enough water to use for drinking and cooking. Some water was used for washing clothes and watering village gardens.

Villagers have meetings at the city hall assembly room in Lakeview. They have community meetings about community concerns and problems. Villagers speak openly to other villagers about plumbing problems, traffic jams, water resources, streets that need repair and educational opportunities, etc.

Jeremy Williams was 47 years old. He was married when he was 23 years old. He had four children. The eldest was 20. The second was 18, the third was 16 and the fourth was 10 years old. Cheryl Williams was 45 years old. She was married to Jeremy Williams. She was the mother of the four Williams' children.

The Williams family was well known in Lakeview, California. Sandra, 20 years old, Jack, 18 years old,

Shelley, 16 years old and Bill, ten years old attended elementary and high school in Lakeview. They participated in school sports, school plays and P.T.A. programs. They went to circuses, carnivals and festivals in Lakeview.

The Williams attended an elementary and high school closest to where they lived. The Williams children had the same teachers in elementary and high school. Sandra, the eldest child, was able to tell her brothers and sister about her teachers. They knew what to expect when they had the same teachers.

The corner grocery store was close to the Williams home. The Williams were able to purchase groceries readily at this grocery store. The Williams could walk down the street to get whatever they wanted such as a gallon of milk and some cookies. They did a little shopping here and there.

At Christmas time the village of Lakeview was decorated and lit up with Christmas decorations. Christmas trees were beautifully decorated and were lit up. They were very interesting to look at. Carolers sang Christmas carols around the village. They went door to door singing a variety of Christmas carols.

They were warmly received by many villagers at their homes.

Other families in the village of Lakeview joined in the Christmas events and festive holidays. Everyone celebrated by attending Christmas parties and other Christmas events.

Villagers in Lakeview had meaningful lives because they related to each other in meaningful ways. They shared community values and activities. They became friends. They believed in village life. They had more purpose for their lives in a village.

FIVE

SURFBOARD PERFORMERS

Surfboard performers must learn to stand properly with coordination while they surf in the ocean on their surf boards. Large, rough, swift waves are dangerous. It takes skill and self confidence to surf across high, swift waves.

Many surfers learn to practice on their surfboards. Regular practice is important to develop strength, control and coordination. They have to concentrate with consistent awareness while surfing across the ocean from wave to wave smoothly without falling off their surfboards.

Waimea Bay is famous in Oahu for surfing on high waves. Surfers catch 30 or 40 foot waves in front of big boulders. They must turn to the right to catch a wave. Timing is important. A surfer cannot wait too long. If a wave breaks on top of a surfer when he or she is paddling out to sea a surfer can be sucked into huge boulders. Surfers can be badly injured. They may even be killed.

Steve Omar is a well known surfer. He has surfed at Waimea Bay and the Pipeline in Hawaii. He has surfed in France, the Bahamas in the West Indies, Tahiti, Bali, Puerto Rico, Mexico, Fiji and Florida.

To prepare for surfing over big waves surfers need training in a municipal, swimming pool. They must learn to swim the whole length of the pool under water back and forth.

Some other well known surfers are Jerry Lopez, Jeff Hackman, Kelly Slater, Andy Irons and Laird Hamilton. They are some of the best surfers in the world. They are capable of surfing over the highest and most dangerous waves in the world.

Surfers must be physically fit in order to surf well. They generally travel to different beaches to surf. They compete with other well known surfers. They have become known to be the best surfers when they compete with other surfing champions.

SIX

THE VACUUM

Joe Hickman was unemployed. He applied for over 50 jobs. He was unable to get a regular job. He had a lot of time on his hands. He was restless and he felt empty.

Joe got up at 10.30 a.m. or 11:00 a.m. each morning. He had difficulty sleeping during the night. He went to bed late at night. He read books to entertain himself.

Day after day went by and Joe tried to overcome the sense of emptiness he felt. He was living in a vacuum. He felt uncertain about his future. He waited to hear from potential employers. He received only one call for a very temporary job.

Joe worked for three weeks as a busboy and host at a restaurant. The work was hard and tiring. He had to carry heavy sacks to the garbage dumps outside. He had to mop the restaurant floors, scrub tables and straighten out tables.

When Joe was finished each night at 11.30 p.m. He was worn out. He had to ride his bicycle 7 miles in the dark to go home. He was completely exhausted from the strenuous labor. Within three weeks Joe was told that he was laid off. The restaurant business had slowed down because summer was over. Tourists had gone home and children had gone back to school.

Joe had a lot of time on his hands again. He rode his bicycle down town. He ate at a sandwich shop during lunch time. He ate a veggie sandwich with soy patties. He read magazines and newspapers in a coffee shop after lunch.

Joe wanted to meet other people in the coffee shop. However, few people came into the coffee shop. So he sat and read to keep busy. He felt lonely because he was used to visiting with many people in Hawaii where he had lived for years. Most of his friends lived in Hawaii.

Joe was a performer. He played the guitar quite well. He was a guitar player and a country singer. He had entertained many people in the past. He wanted to continue to entertain people in public places. Joe had composed 50 songs which he could play on his guitar. There were geese moving in groups in the lagoon. The air was fresh and fragrant from the lagoon.

Joe began to feel much better when he was preoccupied with his music. He was creative and he expressed himself in a meaningful manner.

Joe decided to do volunteer work. He went to the public library to play his guitar and to sing to children. He even read children's books to children. His volunteer work helped him to fill the void. He finally felt less empty. He found fulfillment by doing volunteer work.

SEVEN

MASTER HILARION'S TEACHINGS

Master Hilarion is an ascended master. He has reincarnated many times on Earth. He was St. Paul who lived in Europe. St. Paul lived in Tarsus in Persia. St. Paul was not a Christian at first. In time St. Paul was contacted by Jesus Christ.

Jesus Christ tested St. Paul. St. Paul became blind for a period of time. During his blindness St. Paul began to realize the truths that Jesus Christ exposed. He began to live by universal truths. He purified himself and lived a celibate life.

St. Paul began to preach all over Europe. He formed Christian churches everywhere possible in Europe. Christianity spread throughout Europe. Finally King

Constantine in Turkey maintained Christianity in Constantinople, now renamed Istanbul, the modern, capital city of Turkey. Christianity continued to spread and flourish around the world.

Master Hilarion's previous lives paved the way to his final embodiment on Earth as Hilarian. He was a healer in Greece. He lived a simple life. He meditated frequently to maintain a pure heart force. He helped many people who were ill. He helped them to overcome their illnesses.

Master Hilarion has stated 'Love thy neighbor as thyself.' He focuses on the law of centralization. The law of centralization means the source of light and God's blueprint is in the center of every living creation. Centralization creates unity and oneness. All life begins from the center.

Master Hilarion focuses on karma known as cause and effect. We must overcome negative karma in order to ascend eventually to higher consciousness.

False ties cause negative karma. Positive thoughts and actions help souls to progress on the path. The power of healing is important so that human beings can be healed from negative, imbalanced diseases and karma.

The law of polarity is the law of opposites. Masculine and feminine, positive and negative, up and down, balance and imbalance operate in the law of polarities. The law of transmutation causes purification. Impurities are dissolved and erased.

Love, will and wisdom are a trinity of cosmic principles in The Temple of the People. Matter, force and consciousness are another pattern or trinity. The goal of Templars is to live by cosmic laws and principles. The Ten Commandments are more developed and comprehensive in The Temple of the People.

Service, self sacrifice and self surrender are the keys that awaken a soul to higher consciousness and illumination.

EIGHT

PEACE CORPS SERVICE

The Peace Corps began when President John F. Kennedy established this service organization. The purpose of the Peace Corps is to help the underprivileged countries to learn to become self sufficient.

People in underprivileged countries are trained to become efficient farmers, instructors, engineers, medical assistants, cooks, technicians and to do many other jobs. Trained people are able to improve their countries.

Peace and goodwill can be promoted when underprivileged people are able to improve their living conditions. Self sufficient countries are able to be of service because they are more prosperous and have control over sanitation and social-political issues and problems.

Anna and Jeff Cameron decided to join the Peace Corps. They were in their mid twenties. They were assigned to Kenya in East Africa. They went to a small village out in the southern region of Mount Kilimanjaro in East Africa, where there was a dry climate.

Anna and Jeff had specialized in agriculture and they were excellent farmers. They came to Kenya to teach villagers to become farmers. They showed the Kenyan villagers how to cultivate, water and plant vegetable seeds in desert, jungle soil near the East Coast. They enriched the soil with nutrients and fertilizers so that the villagers could grow a variety of tropical vegetables and fruit trees.

A whole village was able to live off the harvested crops. They harvested squash, corn, beets, potatoes, tomatoes and sweet potatoes. The people in the village were able to eat well. No one starved in the village. Food was stored to be used when new crops were planted.

Anna and Jeff made it possible for children to be vaccinated and inoculated against contagious diseases. They helped to improve sanitation. Water was filtered and purified to prevent contamination. Water must be clean and safe to drink in order to prevent illnesses.

Jeff and Anna also trained the villagers to become mountaineers to be guides for the many tourists coming to climb the challenging Mount Kilimanjaro. Anna also trained villagers to become hosts and hostesses to open hotels and service them.

Other Peace Corps members were assigned to poverty stricken regions in the world. Each Peace Corps worker was assigned to different responsibilities in different, Kenyan villages. They became aware of aids victims. They improved plumbing conditions by installing modern, toilet facilities and bathrooms in homes and public buildings. The improved, modern toilets, showers, bathtubs and running, safe, fresh water made a big difference in improving the health standards.

Oil and gas fields on and offshore were developed on the West African Coast with the help of Peace Corps petroleum engineers. Peace Corps mining engineers also helped to develop the gold and diamond mines in the Kimberly Region. This brought prosperity to Kenya and Uganda when export markets in Europe and America opened up to them.

Villagers and townspeople in East and West Africa have benefited greatly from the service of Peace Corps workers. John F. Kennedy established the Peace Corps. In his famous speech when he was elected President of the U.S.A, John F. Kennedy said, "Ask not what your country can do for you. Ask what you can do for your country."

NINE

WORLD CRISES

World crises exist on Earth. Some major crises are lack of energy, misuse of corporate funds, severe, weather problems causing mass destruction, economic crises, political injustices, loss of food productions and spread of contagious, incurable diseases. World wars have caused enormous, death tolls among our young men and women as well as destruction on Earth.

Political leaders around the world must work together to promote peace and prosperity, make economic progress, formulate social programs and create sufficient jobs. They work for the welfare of the world's people.

Oil and gas are needed around the world. New oil and gas fields are needed on shore and off shore. There is a shortage of petroleum in the western world. Oil from the Middle East has become too expensive. New measures must be taken to ensure that export and import prices are controlled by governments. The present system where private companies and individuals raise the prices must be curbed by government officials. The escalation of petroleum prices this year has caused inflation of the cost of goods and services.

More offshore fields must be discovered like the development of the North Sea oil and gas fields in 1970. The vast North and South Pacific Oceans, The Atlantic Ocean, The Indian Ocean, The Arabian Gulf Seas and The Chinese Seas contain as many petroleum resources as have been discovered in onshore regions of the Earth. Before the development of the North Sea, geologists stated that it was impossible for petroleum resources to exist under the Earth's oceans and seas. Now is the time for vast new oil and gas fields to be discovered. What do the geologists of today say now?

Alternate types of fuel should be experimented with such as hydrogen from water fuel which is inexpensive and does not create air pollution. Fuels from corn, sugar and chemical substances also may be economical. These alternate fuels may help to solve the fuel crisis. Dependence on oil and petroleum from the Middle East is too costly and dangerous.

Food production is scarce in underprivileged countries. There are starving people in India, China and the slums of America. Food is wasted because farmers sometimes produce excessive food that they cannot sell. So they dump the food to rot if they cannot find export markets. This food should be sent to feed the starving millions on Earth. The over population of people in places like India, China and Africa must be controlled by the governments because other countries cannot support billions of people.

Excess food production should be distributed to the needy, hungry masses of down and out people on Earth, such as those in India, Africa and Asian countries. The excess food was too far away to send thousands of miles to people where it was really needed.

Storms, floods, earthquakes and natural disasters have destroyed many cities and towns in different places around the world. Many people have lost their homes and belongings in 2008. Recently Florida and Texas were flooded. As a result, many places were flooded and washed away. Galveston and Houston in Texas were struck with hurricanes. Most homes and other buildings were destroyed in Galveston. It will take years to restore the damage in Galveston. The electricity is still off in many of the states down south in America.

Education is the key to acquiring knowledge, insights and awareness about many subjects and topics. People need a better education in order to learn a profession, business or trade in order to make better and wiser decisions. Education helps to change lives. Wisdom is the way to acquire worthwhile knowledge, goals, purposes and ambitions.

People who acquire skills, knowledge, academic training and schooling tend to be helpful and of service to others. Professors, teachers, doctors, surgeons, librarians, dentists, businessmen and women, inventors, lawyers, political leaders, nurses serve society with their skills and research.

World crises are caused because leaders make wrong decisions and choices and also because masses of people are uneducated. Because of their lack of a proper education and skills they are unable to contribute service in towns and cities or even find employment. These uneducated people become common laborers and many of them are unemployed people. Unemployed people must depend on others to feed them and provide shelter for them. Without help with basic needs many poverty stricken people lie down in the streets and alleys. They have to beg for food or go without clean, fresh food. Underprivileged people tend to become ill and they have contagious diseases. They often pass on their diseases to others. They cannot afford treatments or hospital care. This is a major world crisis. People need employment, clean food and shelter.

Economic crises must be resolved in every nation and country. Nations with natural resources must trade fairly with other less fortunate nations. When the world economies are struggling so that human needs cannot be satisfied many people suffer or die. Irresponsible people who have too many children need to be controlled. The Earth cannot support overpopulated nations such as India, China and some African nations.

If people lose their homes and cannot pay their monthly bills this is because they no longer have enough money. Nations are seriously affected by economic problems which need to be resolved to maintain economic stability.

More progressive goals, objectives and economic progress can make a difference, so that masses of people in each nation can survive and prosper. The government of each nation needs to introduce just laws to control wages, salaries and bonus payments to enable families to have good homes, food and clean water.

World wars and other wars need to be avoided by powerful nations banding together to intervene whenever rulers threaten the peace and stability of the world. All weapons of mass destruction should be banned and destroyed. Terrorists and evil leaders should all be punished for their crimes by their own nations. America and Europe can no longer afford to police the world.

TEN

POLITICAL CHALLENGES

To become a political leader to challenge governmental issues and policies takes diplomacy and effective communications. Politicians need to be prepared to develop policies and bills which are just, effective and helpful to make changes for the better which are needed.

The President of the United States has political challenges to face very frequently. Regulations should be established to stop corruption in government. Misuse of taxpayers' money should be abolished. Taxpayers' money should be carefully used to finance important programs such as energy, agriculture, social services, education, natural resources and maintenance of public services in each state of America.

The President of America is responsible to maintain safety, justice, peace and to promote effective policies and bills to be established to protect American commonwealths and America territories. A President should avoid wars which are unnecessary. He or she must research all viewpoints and information before making important decisions which will affect America and the welfare of the American people.

The American Congress, Senate and House of Representatives should develop effective proclamations, bills and policies to improve the American economy, health and social programs, agricultural growth, educational opportunities and more. The Congress and Senate must vote for or against bills and policies. They strongly affect what changes are made in governmental policies and decisions.

It is challenging for the President and Vice-President to promote new bills and policies if the Congress and Senate vote against new bills and policies. The reverse is possible. The President can veto a new bill and new policy. The bill or policy might not pass if the American President does not cooperate.

He or she has made a difference whether the bill or policy passes.

When presidential candidates are campaigning they must convince voters they have the best policies and can promote effective bills and policies. The presidential candidate needs to be able to speak dynamically and to describe important issues that affect the American nation. Voters want positive changes in governmental programs brought about by innovative and worthwhile policies and bills. The political challenges of the twenty-first century must be resolved and carried out. The President must know how to lead the American people. He or she must know how to run the American government. He or she must stand up and support important and major issues. The challenges are much more demanding each year.

Large companies such as Fannie Mae and Freddy Mack, who have controlled home loans and insurance policies, have become bankrupt. Washington Mutual Bank and Lehman Brothers have gone completely broke. The Federal government has had to pay 85 billion dollars to finance Fannie Mae and Freddy

Mack. The Bank of America has taken over Lehman Brothers and paid approximately 85 billion dollars.

Why have Fannie Mae and Freddie Mack, Lehman Brothers and Washington Mutual have to be refinanced? It is because many middle class people have had their homes foreclosed. They couldn't make the payments. As a result these three financial loan companies went bankrupt. The President made a challenging choice to have the Federal government to pay off two of these companies so they could survive. American tax dollars were used to pay the costs. Our government is 10 trillion dollars in debt. The political challenge made by a Republican President was to risk using federal funds to keep Wall Street afloat.

Now a proposal of 700 billion dollars will have to be used to create a bail-out to save our American economy. American tax dollars will be used to pay the overhead in 2008.

ELEVEN

IMPORTANT PRESIDENTS IN THE U.S.A.

Important Presidents in America have made a difference in the formation of the American government. Their fortitude, vision, endurance and leadership have helped America become strong. Certain American Presidents have made wise decisions when they created effective policies and special deals and concessions to protect America.

George Washington, who was our first American President, fought in the American Revolution to help establish America. American patriots fought alongside George Washington to promote American freedom and liberty from Great Britain.

After the American Revolutionary War George Washington was elected. The first American Congress, Senate and House of Representatives were established. George Washington chose not to become a king. He preferred to be an American president.

The American Preamble and Declaration of Independence were written by Thomas Jefferson, who became our third American President. John Adams, our second American President maintained the American Presidency. He was a strong American President as well. George Washington and John Adams worked closely with the American Congress, Senate and House of Representatives to protect and preserve American laws, patriotism and justice for all.

Thomas Jefferson became the third President of America. He helped form the Declaration of Independence and many laws and bylaws in the American Constitution. He was an educated, cultural person. He formed the first University in America in Virginia. He had explorers travel to the Louisiana Territory. They drew maps and measured the Louisiana landscape. This land became valuable. Pioneers and settlers traveled through the Louisiana Territory. Many of them settled in Louisiana.

Abraham Lincoln was our 16th President of America. He tried to unite the Northern and Southern states. The American Civil War in 1860 through 1865 was fought to stop slavery and corruption in governmental policies in the South. Abraham Lincoln believed in the American dream. He believed in freedom, justice and liberty for all.

Andrew Johnson became the next President after Abraham Lincoln was assassinated. He tried to maintain the American union. He followed Abraham Lincoln's beliefs and policies. Andrew Johnson was attacked for supporting Lincoln's policies and beliefs. He was almost impeached as an American President. He stood up against his enemies. Charles Stevens was his worst enemy. Stevens didn't want to support Lincoln's policies.

Andrew Johnson finally convinced the Congress and Senate after one Senator mentioned he didn't want to have Johnson impeached. Andrew Johnson managed to survive as President of the United States of America. He held the American Union together despite the challenges he faced.

Teddy Roosevelt, who became another President of the United States of America, was an environmentalist.

He believed in preserving the environment. Teddy Roosevelt fought in the Spanish-America War. Americans won that war. California, Arizona and New Mexico became part of America. This strengthened Western states in America.

Franklin D. Roosevelt was President of the U.S.A. for 12 years. A financial recession began in 1929. Roosevelt promoted a New Deal to improve the American economy. He increased more jobs to help Americans to become employed again. He established the 4-H Club and Boy Scouts to foster outdoor activities such as camping, hiking, swimming, 4-H agricultural projects and outdoor survival skills. Scouts learned how to use pocket knives and how to build camp fires and to pitch tents. Boy Scouts learn to fish, hunt and to plant fruits and vegetables. They learn how to take care of livestock, pigs, chickens, turkeys and pets.

John F. Kennedy was our 36th American President. He asked Americans to serve their country. He exposed inflation in America. He formed the Peace Corps to promote world peace and further improvement in living conditions and promote better agricultural methods.

Bill Clinton was an American President for 8 years. He maintained peace. He paid the national debt. He maintained a good economy. He made friends around the world. He tried to improve Social Security and health programs.

The American Presidents who have made a difference have changed America. They have promoted freedom, liberty and justice for Americans. Their patriotism and dedicated service to American democracy has improved the American way of life.

TWELVE

UFO OBSERVATIONS

Much has been said about UFOs known to be unidentified flying objects. UFOs have been seen in many places around the world. They are in a variety of shapes and sizes. Many people have reported UFO sightings.

Recently several people witnessed UFO sightings at Pismo Beach, California. They reported the objects were round and luminous. One of the UFOs dove in the ocean one-half mile near Pismo Beach near the piers.

On August 5, 1608 around 8:00 p.m. many citizens of Nice in France saw three luminous shapes over the Baie des Anges heading at high speed towards their city.

The machines were of a long oval shape, flattened and topped with a sort of mast. Hovering almost motionless, they caused the water beneath them to seethe, giving off a dense orange-yellow vapor accompanied by an infernal noise. From one of the machines a living being emerged, followed by a second.

The outer space beings were human in appearance. They were dressed in red and silver uniforms. Their heads were huge and they had large, round eyes which were luminous. They went into the ocean. Two hours later they came out of the ocean and returned to their spaceships. The spaceships raced swiftly to the east and disappeared.

On August 22, 1608 space visitors appeared at the coast at Genoa in Italy. The Italians in Genoa shot cannons at the UFOs with 800 cannonballs. The spaceships continued to hover in the sky. Eventually, the spaceships moved across the sky and disappeared in the east.

On the morning of November 28, 1954 in Caracas, Venezuela, Gustavo Gonzales and Jose Ponce, two, grocery, delivery men, were making a delivery run in the suburbs in their panel truck. As the two men turned a corner, the two astonished Venezuelans were confronted by a large, luminous, flying saucer which blocked the street. Witnesses stated that the spacecraft was about twenty feet in diameter and rested on three, tripod-type, landing gears.

Gonzales saw an apelike creature which was about four feet tall, walked normally but was covered completely by bristly, black hair. Gonzales picked up this hairy, dwarf-sized creature and carried it over to his truck. The creature whacked him to get away.

The dwarf and other dwarves quickly entered their flying saucers. The flying saucers flew quickly away and disappeared in the sky.

In 1967 on March 8 a group of UFOs was seen flying over Knox County, Illinois by Deputy Frank Courson. The flying saucer made a hissing sound. The saucer-shaped object flew across the sky and disappeared.

On July, 1952 half a dozen UFOs flew over the White House in Washington, D.C. Six UFOs were very visible to many people. They could out-maneuver the American Air Force. These UFO sightings were reported on the 6:00 p.m. television and radio news in America. The Air Force jets went 700 miles an hour. The UFOs went 1,500 miles an hour. People in Washington, D.C. were alarmed.

Albert Einstein called the President of America and begged him not to have the American Air Force attack these UFOs. Einstein didn't want a galactic war to start. The White House might be blown up.

Flying saucers are real spaceships from outer space. The flight patterns and skilled maneuvers of these outer space vehicles indicated they are controlled by intelligent beings. People who have been contacted by outer space beings have tangible evidence that flying saucers may be controlled by humanoids from outer space.

Hundreds of New Jersey residents including public officials, lawmen and newsmen watched as flying saucers hovered for two hours over Wanaque Reservoir on January 12, 1966. Only a few newspapers published the story.

A fourteen-year-old boy, Chris Ward of East Liverpool, Ohio, was temporarily paralyzed by a glowing beam of light from a flying saucer on August 19, 1966. The UFO may have been equipped with heat-blast and paralysis-ray weapons.

Walter Stone, age twenty, of Carlisle, Kentucky had his car buzzed by a fiery UFO on the morning of October 18, 1966. The UFO object was round and made of stone. It had a "powerful invisible force" and it was surrounded by a ring of fire. The UFO hovered very close to his car. He sat low in his car seat.

Sheriffs, deputies and policemen in Ohio pursued a "hot dog" shaped UFO during a wild, eighty-five, mile, interstate chase on April 17, 1966. The saucer stopped often while it was being chased.

A young, Brazilian farmer claimed for several years that he was kidnapped by a crew of outer space, four-foot saucer pilots. He was dragged into their spaceship by a beautiful, space maiden.

Residents of Exeter, New Hampshire, have parked along high-voltage, power lines and watched UFOs swoop in for a nightly recharge. Across the country in Rio Vista, California, townspeople gathered nightly at a water tower to view a reddish, cigar-shaped UFO Lawmen affirmed this incident.

UFOs have been in many countries around the world such as the U.S.A., France, England, Brazil, Italy, Argentina, Australia and many, other countries. There have been many unidentified, flying objects observed by responsible, balanced people in the world.

THIRTEEN

WALL STREET STOCK MARKET CRISIS

Wall Street Stock Market has experienced serious drawbacks because stocks can drop drastically and suddenly at any time. Stocks affect buyers, corporations, business transactions and interest rates.

When stocks go up this affects stock market finances. Stockholders tend to buy stocks that are reasonable. When stocks continue to raise buyers' stocks they receive more financial value. However, when stocks suddenly drop, the value on them goes down considerably.

Corruption has occurred at Wall Street Stock Market in 1929 and now in 2008 because of foreclosures of homes. House payments have gone up too high and monthly house payments have been difficult for middle class people to pay. Many foreclosures have taken place because buyers are unable to make regular payments.

Major corporations have gone bankrupt because regulations have not been established to avoid bankruptcy. Money has been misused and certain individuals and corporate leaders benefited from excessive profits at the expense of the middle class. As a result middle class and lower class people lose out financially because the stock market has gone way down.

Lehman Brothers, Fannie Mae and Freddie Mack, Washington Mutual Bank and several more financial institutions have gone bankrupt in 2008. The American Federal Government and J.P. Morgan Bank have bailed out these financial groups. They paid 83 billion to 85 trillion dollars to save these financial institutions.

What caused these financial institutions to go bankrupt? They didn't set up realistic, financial plans to protect everyone who invests in financial projects and specific investments. They expected investors to use unfixed interest rates to pay higher interests and to receive less personal, interest monies when they invested their money in stocks and some bonds.

Washington Mutual recently borrowed 17 billion dollars. This money was used up and Washington Mutual went suddenly bankrupt. If J.P. Morgan had not paid off the financial losses this bank would have folded, never to open again. This type of financial loss should not happen on Wall Street at the stock market.

The Congress and House of Representatives in Washington, D.C. met at the Capitol Building to establish a new bailout bill which was 110 pages. This bill was put up for a vote on September 28, 2008. The new bill was set up to save the American economy. Millions of Americans have invested in the Wall Street Stock Market. Therefore these people are affected by the worst, financial disaster America has encountered.

This new, bailout bill may help Americans be able to maintain more financial protection. The middle class will be able to sign up for loans. Bank accounts can be maintained and protected by FDIC.

Wall Street Stock Market needs to be changed with new regulations and restrictions to stop corruption on Wall Street at the stock market.

FOURTEEN

DEMOCRATS VERSUS REPUBLICANS

Democrats and Republicans are two, major American political parties in America. These two political parties have different philosophies, policies and way of dealing with political and economic problems and issues.

Republicans believe in getting away from governmental control. Wealthy people establish big enterprises, corporations and money making establishments. They don't believe in strict regulations which would control how much money they make in their businesses. As a result they accumulate very large sums of money or capital.

Republicans frown on American government programs which protect the middle class and lower class. They don't support health insurance programs, Social Security benefits, Medicare, Medical and Social Service programs. Republicans do not focus on the needs of 95% of the American people. They focus on the top 5% of Americans who are wealthy.

Democrats focus on the needs of the middle class and lower class in America. Democrats represent 95% of the American people. Democrats focus on government control by promoting Social Security, Social Welfare, Medicare, Medicaid and healthcare programs. Democrats serve the middle class and lower class, who are 95% of the American people.

Democrats believe in helping anyone who is economically deprived. They help develop social and economic programs to serve the general public. Bill Clinton was a Democrat. He served the American people for 8 years. He preserved the environment, paid the national debt and balanced the national budget. He promoted better education and health programs.

Democrats have promoted peace and goodwill around the world. They have worked for the good of all. John F. Kennedy established the Peace Corps to help underprivileged nations and countries. Democrats serve others who are in need.

FIFTEEN

MARY MAGDALENE MYSTERY

Mary Magdalene lived in Israel during the time Jesus Christ lived in Israel. Jesus began his ministry when he was thirty years old. He preached to crowds and multitudes of Israelites and other cultural groups.

Jesus traveled many miles and he acquired many disciples. He selected twelve disciples who followed him. Mary Magdalene was stoned in the street in Jerusalem. Jesus protected her from being stoned to death.

Jesus forgave Mary Magdalene for her sins. He inspired her to transmute her personal karma. Jesus helped to heal Mary Magdalene. In recent times studies have revealed that Jesus and Mary Magdalene were married and that they had a daughter called Sarah.

When Jesus was crucified in Jerusalem, Mary Magdalene fled out of Israel with their baby daughter, Sarah in a boat. She traveled by boat across the ocean to Europe. She settled in France and developed a village and church. This was the first, Christian church in Europe. Mary Magdalene carried out the teachings of Jesus Christ in France.

There is evidence that Mary Magdalene lived in a small village named Lourdes. Her body was buried near the church. A five-pointed Jewish star is seen on a stone slab. It points to a mystery spot miles away.

Mary Magdalene's bloodline continued through her daughter, Sarah. Sarah gave birth to descendants of Jesus Christ. Mary Magdalene's descendants have continued to multiply in Europe. This noble family has spread Christianity in the Western world.

Mary Magdalene learned many spiritual mysteries from Jesus Christ. She learned about the I Am Presence which is the Father-God and about the Christ Self, who is the Mother-God within. Mary Magdalene became aware of karma, known as cause and effect as well as reincarnation. Reincarnation means each soul re-embodies again to work out karma. Negative karma must be dissolved, erased and transmuted in order to experience purification of the body, mind, spirit, emanations and astral form. Spiritual lessons can be learned in each lifetime.

Mary Magdalene maintained flames of freedom 2,000 years ago in the world. She helped enlighten and illuminate her followers. She lived by the teachings of Jesus Christ. She was aware of her sacred, spiritual centers in her astral and etheric bodies. Mary Magdalene acquired Christhood.

Mother Mary knew Mary Magdalene because she was the mother of Jesus. Mother Mary emanated flames of freedom. She knew many, inner, spiritual mysteries. She spoke to Mary Magdalene about inner mysteries. She protected Mary Magdalene in Israel.

Mary Magdalene carried the sacred flames of freedom in her sacred centers. She continued to maintain these sacred flames of freedom wherever she traveled to. She taught about the spiritual mysteries.

SIXTEEN

TELOS, AN UNDERGROUND DOMAIN

Telos is an ancient, underground city near Mount Shasta in northern California. Telos is a very large, underground city which extends for hundreds of miles. Many underground people live in this enormous, spectacular city.

People who live in Telos come from Lemuria originally. Underground people receive enough oxygen. Many people come from Lemuria and Atlantis. Some of the people come up from the ground below. They mingle among people who live on the surface of the Earth. Then these underground people go back into the Earth to live.

Although the subterranean cities are confined and off-limits for us they serve as a great, protective barrier. Their limitation is our protection. They have allowed our civilizations to flourish these past 12,000 years without any interference at all.

In Telos galactic beings watch over the surface population very carefully, monitoring our movements and reporting back to their councils. They know all that occurs on the Earth's surface.

The underground people say, "We embrace the light as it dawns each day and bless the darkness as it descends on our homes. We bless all of life's activities. We bless this great planet and all its life forms.

"Know that in Telos, we see the light in all its diversity and we use the light's energy to travel in our astral bodies. We use light in all its ramifications to create and develop our civilization underground. Although it may appear dark to you, in reality the underground is quite lit up! Even the tunnel passages glow softly with our crystal light technology.

"When we are underground we are aware of all that takes place in the Universe. We are connected to all star systems in our galaxy via our computer lines, similar to your World Wide Web network. We have a world wide star network that connects all solar systems in our galaxy. We know what star systems all our brothers and sisters are located in and know their current state of evolution by tuning into them on our computers which register all pertinent information through all lifetimes. Our computers are privy to the Akashic Records, and they convert them into readable data."

The underground leader continued by saying, "We know the dark forces have invaded the surface of Earth and are carrying out abductions underground. We know all that occurs on and inside the planet. But had we exposed ourselves we would have been victims also; leaving no one to guard our teachings and technologies or to carry the light."

"In Telos we patiently await this time of increased energy. For it is this elevated consciousness on your part that will allow us to surface. There is a Divine Timing involved here, a Divine Timeframe that will allow us to emerge from our protection under the Earth's surface."

SEVENTEEN

USEFUL INVENTIONS

Inventors are valuable, creative individuals. Their inventions are useful and help improve our way of life. Inventors experiment to discover new inventions. They make a difference in the progress made in different civilizations.

Alexander Graham Bell invented the first telephone. He experimented with cans and metal tubes. He discovered that sound can be projected far away. The telephone is used and has made it much easier to communicate readily.

People are able to call long distance whenever they like to speak to family, friends, business associates, etc. Using a telephone speeds up business transactions as well as personal communications. World communications are more effective with the use of telephones.

The invention of the telegraph added more long, distance communications. The use of a tap system with Morse Code System is used. Messages can be sent many miles away immediately. The telegraph has been especially helpful before the telephone was discovered. The telegraph was the best form of long distance communications.

Eli Whitney invented the cotton gin. The cotton gin has speeded the process of separating cotton to spin cotton into thread. This successful invention has made it possible to collect and process cotton.

Cotton thread has been used to make cotton cloth and other cotton products. Cotton is a reliable plant fiber. It is lightweight and quite durable. Cotton is generally worn during Spring and Summer months.

It is easy to sew with cotton fiber. Many dresses, blouses, shirts, pants and jackets are made of cotton fabrics. Cotton can be dyed in many colors. Bright, cheerful colors are attractive to look at.

Cotton clothing is generally less expensive because it is not made of animal skins. Animal skins tend to be much more expensive. Many people wear cotton clothes.

Household inventions such as toasters, microwaves, miniature ovens, refrigerators, freezers and more are very useful. These inventions help make life much easier for billions of people in their domestic life.

The invention of cars, trucks, vans and jeeps are needed to travel freely wherever drivers travel. These forms of transportation are highly useful so masses of people can travel wherever they want to travel to. Trains, buses, subway trains and streetcars are very helpful and needed for transportation for people who commute to their jobs and back to their homes. Many people do not drive cars. They prefer to ride in a train, on buses, tramways, streetcars and subways.

There are many inventions that have made a difference in the industrial and technological age. Computers and many office machines have been created to use in business, education and for commercial needs. Every new invention can affect our economy, our lifestyles and even our world, well being.

EIGHTEEN

BOOKS AND MORE BOOKS

Many books have been written and published in the world. Books started being published in the 1400s. The Gutenberg Printer was invented and used in Europe. Printed books became popular to read.

There are a variety of books to choose from. Each person can select novels, books, reference books, dictionaries, pamphlets, magazines and newspapers to read. Reading expands our awareness of creative ideas, descriptive details, facts and opinions. As we read intelligent, stimulating information we can learn so much more.

Encyclopedias are quite valuable to use to look up necessary facts, specific details and information.

Reports, theses, essays and research materials are more developed when specific information is used from encyclopedias. Up-to-date encyclopedias such as World Book Encyclopedia, Columbia Encyclopedia, ABC Encyclopedia and other encyclopedias are available to refer to for up-to-date knowledge. Encyclopedias can even be found now on the internet.

Many novels, short stories and articles have been written by authors. Journalists have written a variety of magazine and newspaper articles which are factual, nonfiction messages. Articles describe what, where, who, when and how information which take less time to read.

Novels such as romances, mysteries and science fiction are interesting and worthwhile to read because readers are able to use their imaginations as they read stimulating descriptions, identify with different characters and learn about human interest plots and turning points in each chapter throughout each novel they read.

Commercial and literary fiction books are often longer than nonfiction novels. Authors develop step by step action in their developing story and plots. Turning points and climaxes strengthen the impact of actions and the effect of the turning points and climaxes have on the characters. Readers can become aware of possible life situations, problems, goals and accomplishments which are described in all types of novels.

Poetry books are available at public libraries and bookstores. Some poetry books are in college bookstores. Poetry is very worthwhile to read. Poetic stanzas, colorful, descriptive language and creative thoughts are expressed in poetry. Important messages are expressed immediately in poems. Henry Wadsworth Longfellow wrote a poem <u>Hiawatha</u> which was a narrative, epic poem about the life of Hiawatha, a famous American Indian. Hiawatha united six major tribes in America known as a League of Indian Nations.

Factual books exist in public libraries and bookstores. There are history, biology, mathematics, science and anthropology books which can be located in public libraries and bookstores.

So, enjoy reading books and sharing what your have read in different books. You can benefit from reading a variety of books. There are more and more books available to read.

NINETEEN

MAGAZINE MEMORIES

Magazines exist around the world. There are many magazines such as <u>Saturday Evening Post</u>, <u>Scientific American</u>, <u>National Geographic</u>, <u>Life</u>, <u>Chicago Clarion</u>, <u>The American</u>, <u>Better Homes and Gardens</u>, <u>Time</u> and <u>Look</u>, etc. All are well known magazines.

<u>Saturday Evening Post</u> usually has many human interest stories and news articles. Current issues are covered in different articles. <u>Scientific American</u> has up-to-date scientific achievements and discoveries.

<u>National Geographic</u> has excellent wildlife articles with colorful pictures of different animals. Human interest articles and historical experiences and anthropology discoveries are presented. <u>The American</u>

describes American heroes, leaders and American events.

Life, Time and Look magazines cover stories about celebrities, national leaders, and about other interesting people. Better Homes and Gardens has many pictures of homes and gardens which are desirable to look at. Modern homes which are beautifully and elegantly decorated are quite interesting to enjoy. Reader's Digest is well known for short stories. Many topics are covered.

Magazines provide many, current stories, issues and stimulating topics to read about. Magazines are available at Wal Mart, Rite Aid and in public libraries and at News stands. People are able to read magazines in doctors' offices, dentists' offices and at public libraries. They are delivered to people's homes and in their post office boxes.

We remember many worthwhile stories and feature events which we read about in magazines. Magazines will continue to be displayed in stores and public libraries.

TWENTY

UNUSUAL EPISODES

Roger Templeton was an actor. He had performed in many movies in Hollywood, California. He had main roles in most of the movies he performed in. He was well known and famous as an actor. Roger performed as a cowboy, a soldier, a pioneer and he performed in some science fiction films.

When Roger Templeton rested in his bed he often thought about his acting career. He tended to daydream during the day. Roger dreamt about different movie episodes.

An episode is a narrative digression complete within itself. An episode is any event or series of events complete in itself but forming part of a larger one. Various incidents occur step by step. Roger used his imagination when he daydreamed and dreamt at night. He seemed to be happier when he was thinking of possible experiences he could participate in.

One afternoon while Roger was sitting in his veranda, outdoor porch he began daydreaming. He imagined he was on an expedition in Africa. He entered savannah country. The landscape was dry with sparse, tangled weeds and thick grass.

While Roger Templeton walked through the thick grass with two, expedition companions, Peter and Sam, he heard loud, growling sounds nearby. Suddenly he saw several, female lions ready to pounce on his companions and himself. He realized they would leap very quickly towards him and his companions.

Roger had to think quickly how to protect himself and his companions. He didn't have a gun with him. Fortunately he spotted a dead, tree limb. Roger grabbed the dead limb to defend himself. He quickly used his pocket knife to make a sharp, piercing point on the end of the thin limb.

Roger cut the limb into three pieces and quickly created sharp, pointed ends on the other two, limb parts. The female lions headed towards Roger and his two companions. Roger, Peter and Sam prepared for the attack. They held their pointed limbs like spears. The lionesses pranced close to them.

Roger, Peter and Sam pointed their limb spears at the three lionesses. Each of them directed their spears at a specific lioness. Roger pierced his homemade spear into the closest lioness. He managed to stab the lioness in its forehead. The lioness fell down in pain. Its forehead was bleeding and it was in severe pain. It continued to lie down.

Peter pierced his pointed, homemade spear into another lioness. The spear was pierced into its side close to its heart. The lioness fell to the ground helpless. Sam pointed his spear at the third lioness. He managed to pierce the lioness into its stomach. The lioness finally fell to the ground.

Roger, Peter and Sam observed the three, wounded lionesses on the ground bleeding and in pain. They knew they had to defend themselves. They may have been killed. They continued on their expedition to get away from the bloody ordeal they had just experienced.

Roger stopped daydreaming and recognized himself in the veranda, outdoor porch. He was relieved to be safe in his own home.

Roger was quite busy most of the time reviewing dialogue for his next movie. He was assigned to the roll of the king in <u>The King And I</u>. He practiced his lines over and over to prepare for rehearsals with the acting team. <u>The King And I</u> would be performed in three weeks.

When Roger finished practicing his lines he decided to go down to a nearby lake. He walked along the embankment and felt a cool breeze blow against his face and body. He felt relaxed as he walked near the cool, dark, blue lake.

Suddenly a surfer was gliding with a wind sail on the lake. The surfer lost control and moved on his surfboard very close to the shore. In fact, the surfer slid out of the lake and hit Roger. Roger felt the full impact of the surfer because he was struck so hard by the surfer. Roger was injured. His ribs and left arm were broken. He was in physical shock from his injuries.

The surfer fell to the embankment close to Roger. His heavy surfboard landed on the ground nearby. Roger continued to lie there in pain. Finally, someone came by and noticed that he was lying there injured. The observer used her cell phone to call an ambulance.

When an ambulance arrived at the scene of the accident, paramedics brought a stretcher to put Roger in. He was wrapped in warm blankets after he was checked over. The surfer was checked over as well and put in the ambulance. The ambulance driver drove Roger and the surfer to the nearest hospital. They were taken to the Emergency Ward.

Roger's broken ribs would have to heal without any doctor's treatment. A doctor reset his broken, left arm. Roger wore an arm brace after his left arm was carefully wrapped. He was still in severe pain. He didn't expect to be injured especially at the edge of the lake.

The surfer who caused the accident had bruises and cuts on his body. Both Roger and the surfer, known as Ramos, stayed in the Emergency Ward for several hours to rest from the shock of being in an accident.

Finally, Roger and Ramos were allowed to leave the hospital. Roger went home to his apartment. Roger would have to recover before he could act in movies or on stage again. It took three months for his ribs to heal. It took approximately six months for his left arm to heal.

Once Roger had recovered from the accident he was able to go back to work. However, he had to give up the role of being the king in <u>The King And I</u>. He was disappointed he was unable to act in <u>The King And I</u>. He hoped to have an opportunity to act in a leading role in a well known movie or stage play.

TWENTY-ONE

POTTERY MAKING

Pottery has been created for thousands of years. Ancient civilizations such as Lemurians, Atlanteans, Sumerians, Babylonians, Egyptians and Europeans knew how to make pottery. They made large flower vases with clay. They also produced water pitchers, plates, cups, saucers and many more objects with red and brown clay.

Learning the art of pottery making takes practice. It takes a lot of experience on a regular basis to become a skillful potter. Pottery is generally painted on the different pottery. Colorful designs add to the beauty of the pottery.

Artistic pottery is made all over the world today. Pottery is especially popular in Italy, Spain, Portugal and Mexico. Pottery is popular in New Mexico, Arizona and California in America.

A potter's wheel is needed. Clay is mixed and placed on the potter's wheel. The clay is shaped as it spins around on the potter's wheel. It is carefully shaped as the wheel moves around.

Ancient pottery is considered to be very valuable. Many ancient vases, jars, bowls and dishes made of clay are displayed in museums around the world. They are appreciated by many people.

Many people display flower pots, vases, jars, dishes and cups in their homes and gardens. Large, flower pots are put in gardens and even in public, cultural centers. Large, flower pots and vases are seen in Santa Barbara, California. Many flower pots are seen in San Diego, California.

Pottery making is a cultural art and special, artistic skill. It takes artistic talent and special coordination to produce quality, lasting pottery. Pottery making is worth experiencing as an avocation or hobby.

TWENTY-TWO

INTELLECTUAL PEOPLE

Intellectual people are very interested in ideas, facts and concepts beyond ordinary thoughts. They usually specialize in given subjects and do research about intellectual ideas. An intellectual person absorbs multiple ideas and factual information.

Henry Harrison was an intellectual person. He was an enthusiastic reader. He read constantly and learned about many things. He was intellectually inclined in junior high school, high school and college.

Henry was capable of preparing well developed research projects. He could talk about subjects in great detail and depth. He was eager to learn more and more. Henry could expand his thoughts and express specific examples and facts about a given topic.

Henry joined in intellectual discussions such as group discussions about literature, anthropology, social issues, religious philosophies, scientific discoveries, experiments and historical knowledge, etc.

Intellectual people generally like to communicate about what they have learned regarding their readings and research. They continue to acquire more and more knowledge. Some intellectual people acquire wisdom as they absorb knowledge. They use their intuition and go within to examine and become enlightened because of what they have learned from books and ideas.

The more a person learns from books as well as television and discussion groups helps this person to share what he or she has learned. Knowledge should be shared with others.

TWENTY-THREE

AMBITIOUS PEOPLE

Ambitious people have specific goals and expectations. They decide what they want to achieve. Usually an ambitious person receives a specific education and training to prepare for the occupation they choose to do. Step by step goals are achieved to accomplish their goals and objectives.

Jan Morrison decided to become an interior decorator. She went to college to major in interior decorating. After five years of college Jan received a B.A. in Interior Decorating. She had learned to decorate houses and apartments with interesting wallpaper and painted walls. She selected stylish furniture and window curtains to match the décor in each house and apartment.

Customers called Jan Morrison to come decorate their homes. Each customer told Jan what they wanted done in their home. Jan did her best to meet their desires. She was very successful as an interior decorator.

Larry Shoemaker was an ambitious person. He wanted to become a college professor. He majored in English. He had studied English literature in high school, college and graduate school.

Larry read many, well known books about the works of Shakespeare, Shelley, Keats, Browning, Louisa May Alcott, Charles Dickens, Jane Austen, Tennessee Williams, Daniel Defoe, Charlotte Bronte, Henry Wadsworth Longfellow, Ralph Waldo Emerson, Henry David Thoreau, George Bernard Shaw and many more authors.

While Larry Shoemaker was attending college he continued to read and study the writings of many, well known authors. He wrote essays, theses and reports about different authors. When he went to graduate school he continued to learn more and more about English literature. He did very well throughout college.

Larry Shoemaker received his B.A. and Ph.D. in English Literature. He applied for a college professor's position at the University of Colorado in Denver, Colorado. He went for an interview in the English Department. The interviewer asked him many questions about what techniques he planned to use to teach English Literature. After the interview Larry was contacted in several weeks. He was told that he received the position as an English Literature professor at the University of Colorado.

Larry packed his luggage and traveled by air to Denver, Colorado. He attended the introductory seminar. Then he was given his course schedule. He was assigned to four classes in English. He would teach English 102, 102, 103, and 104.

Larry Shoemaker created his syllabus for each course. He developed his goals and objectives for each course. The college students at the University of Colorado signed up for his English classes. Larry clarified his goals and objectives very well. He passed the syllabuses out in each course clearly.

Larry was a successful, college professor for many years. He related well to college students and helped many of his students do well in their English courses.

Ambitious people usually succeed in the things they want to do. They are determined to do well in their chosen occupations and avocations. People like Henry Ford, Albert Einstein, Thomas Edison, Henry Wadsworth Longfellow, Ralph Waldo Emerson and many more people were ambitious people. They were very successful people. They were well known for their ambitious pursuits.

TWENTY-FOUR

GOURMET COOKS

Gourmet cooks have special training in order to prepare many, gourmet meals. They generally receive specific recipes with gourmet foods.

Rich sauces and spicy sauces make gourmet food taste good. How the food is arranged on each plate helps to make the food look more interesting and more desirable to eat.

Meat tastes much better when savory, beef stock and chicken, stock juices are spread into the meat. Tasty, juicy meat adds to the gourmet flavor in the meat. Meat is cut up in an interesting way. The meat is placed in a platter in a certain manner to appear sumptuous.

Gourmet cooks generally place food step by step on top of one another. Sautéed vegetables are placed on a plate. Prepared meat is placed over the sautéed vegetables. Mashed potatoes or sliced potatoes go on top of the meat. Then spices and sauce are spread on top of the platter of food. The special arrangements and style of food arrangements make a difference in the taste and effect the gourmet food has on the eater.

Salads can be prepared with gourmet ingredients. Gourmet ingredients include salsa sauce and corn kernels, olives, guacamole dip and several types of lettuce, spicy dressing with herbs plus beans and sliced chicken. Many exotic, very tasty salads can be created. Add sliced avocados, tomatoes, carrots and green peppers to your salad.

Stuffed tomatoes with tuna and celery are delicious. Gourmet cocktail dishes are very tasty. Shrimp and tomato sauce with cut celery taste very good.

Lamb stew is rich in taste. Lamb meat has a special flavor. Lamb meat blends with cooked potatoes, carrots, string beans and corn. A rich, meat sauce adds to the lamb stew. You can eat delicious cornbread with your lamb stew. This lamb stew and cornbread with melted butter is a very delectable meal.

Enjoy gourmet cooking. You will benefit from gourmet cooking.

TWENTY-FIVE

OCEANSIDE ADVENTURES

Adventures at the seaside can be exciting. Many oceanside settings are worth viewing. There are a variety of life forms drifting on the beach. As a person walks on the beach he or she can observe dead seaweed, driftwood, a variety of shells such as sand dollars, clam shells, scallop shells and nautilus shells.

Many beach roamers collect as many shells as they can take back home. They display their collection of shells around their front and back yards. Shells can be arranged on porch ledges and against walls.

Dogs run on the beach. They chase seagulls, pelicans and sandpipers. Dogs run into the ocean and swim in the currents. Waves splash over the dogs as they run in the ocean water. Dogs like to bark when they get excited.

People are seen lying on the beach on large towels. They lie there sunning themselves. Some people get sunburned because they lie on the beach too long.

A person can roam on a beach close to the ocean. It is fun to walk barefoot on the wet sand and feel the warm, sand particles on one's feet. Waves splash to shore onto the strollers who are walking near the ocean.

Many beach roamers stop to make sand castles on the beach. The sand castles may be large or small. Some sand castles look very real and elaborate. Children like to play on the beach. They make sand castles. They cover in sand up to their heads. The warm sand is totally covered over them. They need help getting out of the sand.

Some people have picnics on the beach. They bring sandwiches, potato chips, cut vegetables, cake, cookies and drinks. They put a big towel or blanket on the beach. Picnic food is placed on the blanket which generally is in baskets or brown sacks.

Families, couples, groups and children sit on the beach. They observe the ocean. Sometimes there are sailboats, surfers and people dressed in swimming suits in the ocean. It is interesting to watch the many activities going on in the ocean.

Oceanside adventures vary and people enjoy participating in volleyball games. They play catch with balls. They go swimming. Their adventures on the beach are worthwhile.

TWENTY-SIX

MUSICAL INSTRUMENT TUNERS

Piano tuners are able to tune many pianos. They are able to tune Baldwin, grand pianos, Steinway, grand pianos, upright pianos, clavichord pianos, etc. As long as they have piano keyboards to tune they are able to tighten or loosen piano strings.

Each string represents a piano tone or note. There are many bass and higher notes. A piano tuner has developed the skill of adjusting each key so each key produces the correct tone. Accurate tones must be produced so piano notes are in tune.

Some piano tuners are blind. Yet they are capable of tuning pianos. Blind people have better hearing. So, they are able to tune pianos.

Pianos must be tuned regularly to keep them in good shape. A quality, high grade piano is wonderful to listen to. A Steinway piano is one of the finest pianos to listen to. Steinway was able to select quality wood, quality strings and create well built keyboards.

Mozart played on a clavichord piano. He composed his piano compositions on a clavichord piano. His pieces sounded good on the clavichord. They can be played on pianos as well.

Without quality pianos and clavichord turners these keyboard instruments would eventually sound out of tune. It is important to keep these keyboard instruments in tune so they will sound good.

Guitars, violins, violas, cellos and bass violas must be tuned frequently. The strings must be tightened in all of these instruments. To keep each string instrument tuned is important. When each musical instrument is properly tuned they sound good. Professional musicians check to see if their string instruments are properly tuned so they will sound harmonious. They are able to produce quality, sounding music.

TWENTY-SEVEN

LAURA'S NEW JOB

Laura Henderson had just completed high school. She didn't have enough money saved to go to college. So, Laura decided to look for a job. She was healthy, attractive and capable of doing manual tasks.

Laura was capable of sweeping floors, washing dishes, cleaning tables, waiting on tables and emptying garbage. Laura was capable of mopping floors. She was intelligent enough to write customer orders in order tablets.

Several waitress positions were available in the town Laura Henderson lived in. She applied at three restaurants for a waitress position. She was dressed in a blue, cotton dress with white shoes. Her red, curly hair was combed neatly. She was slender and she had blue eyes.

Laura was interviewed by the boss of each restaurant that had a job position. She was asked questions. Laura answered each question carefully. The interviewer asked, "How old are you? Have you been a waitress before? Demonstrate how to write a food order." Laura was shown a menu. She was given codes for each food. Laura demonstrated a code for chicken with baked potatoes, vegetables, soup and a cold drink. Laura wrote the abbreviated code for this order. She wrote the order accurately.

All three restaurant owners and interviewers were impressed with Laura. She was offered a waitress position at a coffee shop called Sam's Place. Laura was asked to work from 12:00 a.m. to 8:00 a.m. which was the night shift. She accepted this waitress position.

Laura's new waitress position would prove to be challenging. She had never been a waitress before. She was required to buy a waitress uniform. She wore her new uniform to work. She came ten minutes early the first couple of nights.

Another waitress showed Laura how to become a waitress. Laura set all the tables in her section. She studied the menu carefully so she would be able to write the customer orders correctly. Laura brought cold water to tables when customers arrived. She handed out menus to customers.

Laura walked over to customers' tables to ask what customers wanted to order. Customers made decisions about what they wanted to order. Laura wrote down their orders in her menu pad. She listed the cost of food next to each order of food. Laura made a few mistakes while she listed the food items.

Many customers came in around 12:30 a.m. There was only one other waitress on duty. Sam's Place was a very large restaurant. Laura had to serve ten booths. Eight, separate groups came into Sam's Place. Laura rushed to one table after another to bring fresh, cold water. She rushed to each table to write down each order.

It was challenging for Laura to serve eight, separate tables. Laura tried very hard to bring the food to each table. She had to bring bread, soup and salad to many customers. She kept rushing to bring the food. The main orders were put on a counter near the cook's station. Laura managed to bring two or three orders on a tray.

Laura tried to remember who selected specific orders. She asked the customers what their orders were. She placed each order on the table.

Laura managed to serve 24 people within 30 minutes. Each table waited approximately 10 minutes each to receive their food. Some customers were impatient. They didn't like to wait. Some customers ordered milk shakes. Some ordered banana splits.

Laura had to be shown how to make milkshakes and banana splits. She took more time as she learned to prepare milkshakes and banana splits. The customers appeared to enjoy them.

Some customers ordered breakfast specials. Sam's Place was known for making delicious breakfasts. Scrambled eggs, hash browns, ham, sausages and bacon were served with the eggs and potatoes. Pancakes, biscuits and toast were served with the breakfast food. Syrup and butter were served with the pancakes.

Laura came to each table to serve caffeinated or decaffeinated coffee. She also served Lipton, hot tea and iced tea. She brought more water for those who requested it.

Laura continued to clean empty tables. She collected dirty dishes, silverware, used napkins, cups, saucers and glasses. She cleaned off each table with a wet cloth. She wiped each table with a dry cloth. She checked for food droppings on the floor at each empty table.

As each group of customers left they asked Laura to take their money up to the cashier register. She brought back the change. Some customers left good tips. Some customers didn't leave a tip. Laura collected the tips from the tables she served.

At 8:00 a.m. Laura was allowed to go home. She was exhausted because she had worked hard from 12:00 a.m. to 8:00 a.m. Her feet and legs were aching. She was tired. She was glad to go home. She added up her tips and put them in her purse.

The manager smiled at Laura as she was preparing to go home. The manager said, "You have worked hard. I know this was your first evening. Go home to rest. I'll see you tomorrow night." Laura smiled back at the manager. She was glad that he praised her especially on her first assignment at Sam's Place. She hoped she would do as well or better the next night.

TWENTY-EIGHT

NOVELTIES

There are many novelties to look forward to experiencing. A novelty is a special attraction. Going to a circus can be an exciting experience.

Children look forward to going to a circus, fair or bazaar. These novelties are stimulating and adventuresome for adults as well. Children enjoy riding on a Ferris wheel. They enjoy cotton candy and hot dogs.

Circus stunts are very exciting to observe. Aerialists swing on high wires and risk their lives to do risky stunts. Some have a net under the wires. If an aerialist slips and falls he or she can fall into a net below. The audience becomes frightened and very concerned when an aerialist slips and falls into a net.

If a net has not been put under the high wires the acrobats had to be very careful not to fall. If they fell to the floor they could be badly injured or killed. The audience becomes fascinated when they observe different, risky stunts. Some aerialists move across to a burning hoop and go through it. This excites the audience.

There are many novelties at State Fairs. Bands and music groups entertain at State Fairs. There are booths with prizes of all kinds such as stuffed animal toys, trinkets, jewelry, dolls, miniature statues, etc. Children and adults win prizes after they throw small balls into holes and openings. If they get three balls in the ringers they win prizes. These novelties are stimulating and exciting.

Talent shows are presented such as humorous skits, dancing stunts and musical performances. Children and adults are entertained when they attend talent shows, dancing stunts and musical performances.

Elephants, giant horses and pigs as well as goats, donkeys and zebras are exciting to observe. Children are allowed to touch animals at State Fairs. They are allowed to feed animals. They become involved as they feed and pet animals.

Novelties include sewing bees, eating pies and observing flowers in a special room. Special, flower displays are exciting to observe. Jewelry displays and paintings are exciting to display.

So, enjoy different novelties. It is fun to look forward to different adventures and novelties.

TWENTY-NINE

KARMIC SITUATIONS

We encounter karmic situations every day. We must face negative as well as positive karma. How we do face karma which is cause and effect. Negative karma can affect how we feel. We can be pulled down by negative karma. Positive karma generally helps us feel better about ourselves and others.

Negative karma makes us react with negative emotions such as fear, dislikes, hate, resentments, doubt, malice and anger. When someone mistreats you, you become angry and feel hurt. If you can forgive mistreatments and detach yourself from your reactive mind you can free yourself from negative emotions and attachments.

Negative karma can cause imbalances and diseases in one's body and mind. Positive karma uplifts you. Laughter, joy, cheerfulness, harmonious situations and loving responses are all part of positive karma. Positive karma helps produce balance and better health.

We can change our karma. Karmic situations alter our lives. We can change our circumstances. We can feel better about ourselves and others.

Positive karma uplifts us and helps us so that wise decisions and choices are made. Wise choices change our lives. We may select better jobs and attend better schools. More opportunities for a better life can take place. People with better opportunities in life are much happier and usually well adjusted.

Successful, well known people have chosen to succeed in whatever they can do best. Grace Kelly, Carey Grant, Jane Powell, Elizabeth Taylor, Gene Kelly, Benjamin Franklin, Thomas Jefferson, Franklin Roosevelt and many, other successful people have paved their way to success and happiness.

Successful, well adjusted people have positive goals and objectives. They are achievers and they accomplish what they set out to do. Their karmic experiences help them to expand their awareness about many things in the world.

THIRTY

JAPANESE GARDENS

Japanese gardening is a special type of gardening. Japanese people develop gardens with ponds, bonsai trees and many green plants. Pathways are cultivated through their gardens.

Generally Japanese bridges are put in garden ponds so the Japanese families can walk over the bridges. The bridges create freedom to walk over the ponds.

Japanese gardens are important to Japanese people. They believe in surrounding themselves with a beautiful nature setting. They worship Shinto gods. They place religious statues in their gardens. Beautiful settings produce a peaceful environment.

Many Japanese gardens have five-tiered pagodas which are religious shrines. Each tier represents nature elements of fire, air water and earth. Japanese people worship nature elementals and spirits.

Japanese tea ceremonies are performed in Japanese gardens. The women of the household prepare Japanese green tea. They place small cups on Japanese trays. Teapots are used for the green tea. Once guests and relatives are seated in Japanese gardens green tea is served first to men and boys. Women and girls are served last.

Japanese, religious chants are performed in Japanese gardens. These religious chants are spoken to worship Shinto gods and nature spirits.

Japanese gardens are cultivated in a central location near each Japanese house. Japanese houses are made of wood and tiles. Paper walls are put inside the houses. A special room is reserved to display special paintings and flowers. Other household plants exist in certain places in Japanese homes.

Japanese people perform Japanese tea ceremonies frequently. They also sit in their Japanese gardens quietly to meditate silently. In their Japanese gardens they are able to relax, appreciate nature and to continue to pray to their Shinto gods.

THIRTY-ONE

THE COUNTRY HAY RIDE

In the countryside in many regions there are farms where hay is grown. The hay is harvested and put in hay wagons and trucks. It is the custom to enjoy country, hay rides once hay is harvested and gathered.

People in small villages generally go on country, hay rides. Several horses are hitched to a big wagon. Hay is placed abundantly in the wagon. Generally a group of people dress casually and wear straw hats to protect themselves from the sunlight.

Bill, Cindy, Susan and Charley decided to go on a hay ride in the countryside. They prepared a picnic lunch. Cindy and Susan made ham and cheese sandwiches. They added lettuce, tomatoes and pickles.

Mayonnaise and mustard were spread on sourdough bread. The sandwiches were cut in half. Cindy made apple pie, which she put into the big, picnic basket. Susan prepared potato salad with cut, boiled potatoes, mayonnaise, cut celery, parsley and boiled, chopped eggs.

Once the picnic basket was ready Cindy, Susan, Bill and Charley stepped into the hay wagon near the barn on Bill's farm. Bill and Charley sat up in a driver's seat to guide the horses. Cindy and Susan sat in the hay in the wagon. While the horses were moving the hay wagon Cindy, Susan, Bill and Charley saw meadows of grass, lupines, poppies, trees and bushes. The scenery was very scenic and the air was refreshing with the scent of wild flowers and grass.

Sunshine filtered through oak trees and pine trees into the hay wagon as it moved under shady trees. The shade helped cool Cindy, Susan, Bill and Charley off. They continued on their journey into the countryside. They came to a creek with running water. Before they passed the creek Bill and Charley stopped at the creek so the horses could drink creek water.

Finally, Bill and Charley came to a giant, oak tree after they left the creek. They decided to stop near the giant, oak tree to have their picnic lunch. Bill and Charley tied their horses near the oak trees. Cindy, Susan, Bill and Charley got out of the hay wagon.

Cindy and Susan took the picnic basket out of the hay wagon and they put a big blanket on the ground under the big, oak tree. Once the blanket was spread under the tree they took the picnic food out of the basket to put on the blanket. Cindy passed out sandwiches to everyone. Susan served potato salad on paper plates. Bill passed out cold drinks to everyone. Charley passed out napkins and plastic forks. Everyone began eating their sandwiches, potato salad and they drank their cold drinks.

Bill spoke first. He said, "I haven't stopped here before." Cindy said, "This giant, oak tree must be over several hundred years old. It could be one thousand years old. It is still standing!" Susan said, "There are many oak trees in California. We are fortunate to live in California because it is one of the productive places in the U.S.A."

Cindy said, "I grew up in California near this valley. I like it here. I want to remain in this area. The weather is generally pleasant here." Bill replied, "I have my farm here. I am planning to maintain my farm. I can grow hay, barley, oats and even corn." Cindy, Susan and Charley thought about what Bill said.

Whippoorwills, black crows and sparrows were flying near the giant, oak tree. The whippoorwills and sparrows were chirping. Their bird sounds were pleasant to listen to. The black crows cawed loudly.

Everyone continued to eat their picnic lunch. A pleasant breeze blew around them. They were relaxed by the shady, oak tree and cool breeze. After lunch Susan served apple pie to everyone. The apple pie was very delicious. When lunch was over everyone helped to clean up. The picnic leftovers were put away in the basket. The blanket was folded and put in the hay wagon.

Cindy, Susan, Bill and Charley got back in the hay wagon. Susan put the picnic basket in the wagon before she sat in the hay. Bill and Charley started the hay wagon by holding the reins to guide the horses. They headed back to Bill's farm which was seven miles north.

Once the hay wagon was headed on the road back toward Bill's farm Cindy and Susan sang folk songs. Bill and Charley joined in. They sang <u>Old Black Joe</u>, <u>The Virginia Reel</u>, <u>Red River Valley</u> and more folk songs.

After a while clouds appeared in the sky. Eventually it began to rain. Bill, Charley, Cindy and Susan became dripping wet with rain. The rain felt cold. Wind made it colder. They wanted to get home as fast as they could.

Several hours later Bill, Charley, Cindy and Susan returned to Bill's farm. They all were cold and wet. They went into the farmhouse to change their clothes and to warm up after they became dry again. They hoped to go on another hay ride in the future. They hoped it wouldn't rain when they were in the open wagon.

THIRTY-TWO

THE PUB

Many adults like to go to pubs to unwind. They go to relax, drink and visit with other customers. They joke, laugh and listen to jukebox music or small, music groups. They watch sports and news on televisions.

The local pub is a place to socialize, dance and to drink. People should not over drink especially if they are driving a car home after they leave a pub.

The movie Cheers is about people who go to a pub. They joke, laugh and enjoy relating to other people in the pub. Even employees laugh, joke and socialize in pubs. They serve alcoholic drinks and listen to the customers.

Some customers go home feeling better and more relaxed. Other customers go home drunk and inebriated. They need to be driven home because they have had too much to drink.

Pubs have been around for a long time. Pubs exist in Great Britain, Europe, America, Canada and Australia. They probably will continue to exist for many years to come.

THIRTY-THREE

PROFICIENT LINGUISTS

Individuals who study different languages and learn to speak foreign languages are very valuable on Earth. Linguists are able to translate languages at the United Nations Building and General Assembly in America. They are able to translate readily and communicate with efficiency in English, Spanish, French, German, Italian, Russian and Chinese, etc.

Usually linguists have learned at least two or three languages quite well. It is significant to have knowledge and develop the ability to speak fluently in specific languages. When major, political leaders attend important meetings at the White House in Washington, D.C. people from other countries come.

These people from other countries speak foreign languages. Interpreters translate their messages so political leaders can understand what they are communicating.

Influential, political leaders need interpreters to help them deliver political, effective communications. Effective communication is vital so that positive, political policies can be developed to promote world peace, better environments, positive social and scientific programs.

Major decisions are made by political leaders that help humanity because of the decisions they make. Natural resources are preserved and used wisely. Food is traded and sent to people who need nutritious food.

Wars can be avoided if world leaders communicate effectively. Translators help world leaders to avoid wars because of translations of worthwhile messages to solve misunderstandings and differences. Most problems can be resolved without war.

Linguists are worthwhile in the world. They make a difference in communicating important decisions to improve life on Earth. Linguists are capable of protecting people in different locations on Earth because they can communicate in different languages.

Linguists use headphones to listen to someone who speaks in foreign languages. They repeat the messages they receive in English to those people who speak English. Other languages are also translated from English to other languages.

THIRTY-FOUR

DELEGATES AT THE UNITED NATIONS

The United Nations is located in New York City near the harbor. The UN Building is a large skyscraper with many windows. There are many departments and services to help needy people who are starving and suffering from diseases.

There are such organizations as CARE Incorporated, the Peace Corps, UNESCO, World Health Organization, World Bank and many more, service groups. The CARE Organization sends food and supplies to underprivileged countries.

The United Nations was established to promote world peace, prosperity in all countries and to create protection for underprivileged people. The United

Nations is a place where world leaders, delegates and the UN Council meet to discuss major, world issues. World leaders try to find ways to make positive changes.

The UN Assembly assembles to develop economic sanctions, policies and proclamations to use to change world conditions. Sally MacDonald and Gerard Jones were UN delegates. They attended UN Assembly meetings to participate in discussions about political and economic policies and sanctions.

Sally MacDonald spoke and could translate in English, French, German and Italian. She even understood some Russian and Chinese language. Sally promoted a policy which was about developing ways to avoid waste of food. She stated, "Oranges and apples should not be wasted because of price changes. All farm crops should be sent to grocery stores and used in food chains. Extra fruit, vegetables, grain, etc., should be given to needy people."

Sally MacDonald strongly promoted her written policy to the World Health Organization. She encouraged delegates in the UN Assembly to vote for this policy. The UN Assembly was asked to vote for this positive, food policy. 185 UN delegates voted yes. 46 UN delegates voted no. This new policy was passed.

Sally MacDonald continued to develop other policies and proclamations to improve world conditions. She developed a bill to promote better, educational methods in the schools. She stated, "Worthwhile and progressive, educational supplies should be purchased to use in every classroom." Sally suggested ways to accumulate money and other funds to pay for educational supplies. Quality educational tools are necessary to use to teach students.

Gerard Jones promoted UN policies to improve agricultural methods in impoverished countries. There are needs for tractors, modern ploughs, vegetable cultivators, harvesters and more farm equipment. Gerard Jones developed a UN policy to protect masses of people from harmful germs. He stated, "Harmful germs cause many diseases. Special medications must be developed to prevent AIDS, cancer and other diseases."

Gerard Jones presented his policies to the UN Assembly. The UN delegates voted. 197 UN delegates voted yes about agricultural methods and agricultural tools to be used in impoverished countries. 23 UN delegates voted no. So, this policy was passed. Gerard's policy about eliminating harmful germs was also passed in the World Healthcare Assembly.

Sally MacDonald and Gerard Jones met in the UN Assembly Hall. They spoke about UN policies. Sally and Gerard became good friends. Both of them were single. Gerard decided to ask Sally out for dates. She accepted Gerard's dates.

Gerard took Sally out to dinner and to Broadway shows in New York City. They ate at a variety of restaurants. They both enjoyed Chinese food, Italian dishes, French food and American food. Sally and Gerard went to other activities in New York City. They went to Art museums and galleries and to Chinatown. They went on harbor cruises. They saw the Statue of Liberty in New York Harbor.

All in all, Sally and Gerard had a wonderful time in New York City. They continued to work as delegates at the United Nations. They continued to develop more policies and proclamations to help humanity around the world.

THIRTY-FIVE

RESPIRATORY PROBLEMS

Respiratory problems exist because people develop colds, mucus buildup and viruses. They may come down with pneumonia or bronchitis, etc. Respiratory problems are difficult to overcome.

Viruses are generally dormant in a person's body. If a person becomes weak and becomes exposed to virus germs this person can come down with colds, pneumonia or bronchitis. It is difficult to breathe when a person has a stuffy cold, bronchitis or pneumonia.

Specific medications must be used to help a person to get well. Antibiotics are used to treat diseases. It may take weeks or months to become well again.

Avoid eating foods that cause mucus. Milk, cheese, cream, butter and eggs tend to cause mucus problems. Mucus must be cleared from bronchial tubes, a person's throat and breathing passages. A person should clear his or her throat and take medication to clear physical congestions.

Respiratory problems can be cured if a person breathes fresh air. Walking regularly and breathing deeply help to clear the respiratory tract. Viral germs can be stopped by people continuing to take antibiotics, eating properly and exercising regularly.

Ninety-six percent of people with sinus problems have hidden fungus in their mucus. Every day your nose and sinuses produce two cups of mucus. It comes out of your sinuses into your nose and then down the back of your throat where it's swallowed. This happens automatically so you don't notice anything.

Researchers at the Mayo Clinic have studied 210 patients with chronic sinusitis. Using new methods of collecting and testing mucus from the nose, researchers discovered fungus in 96% of the patients' mucus. Flora Sinus helps to trigger a positive immune response in you that then attacks your fungi, helping to reduce the inflammation it causes.

You can end painful inflammation, soreness and tenderness by ending swelling and deep mucus buildup that causes congestion and a runny nose. You can clear out the encrusted fungus that lines your nasal passages. It helps you breathe without congestion, pain, swelling, headaches and irritation.

There are between 400 and 500 strains of respiratory conditions. Much of sinusitis has to do with the failure of the immune system to deal effectively with stressors that bombard everybody's sinuses every day. Air pollutants, smoke, dust and dust mites, mold, mildew, pet dander, pollen, viruses, bacteria and fungi cause respiratory problems.

The Nutri Health Seasonal support entitled Flora Sinus works for you. You can call 1-800-914-6311 to order Flora Sinus. Forget about drugs that promise everything and deliver at best temporary relief.

Two extraordinary researchers, Ulrich Gluck and Jan Olaf Gebbers have made a difference regarding ways to improve respiratory problems. You will find these four medically proven powerhouses in Flora Sinus. This ground-breaking research made headlines around the world because it was co-sponsored by the enormously respected Institute of Pathology and Environmental Medicine in Luzerne, Switzerland.

The world-famous Nobel Prize Organization reveals that once your immune system is turned on, invaders don't "stand a chance." The Nobel Prize Organization says your immune system could make you "100 times safer once it's operating at full strength. There are very few hostile organisms that stand a chance."

Four probiotics in Flora Sinus help turn on and power up God's greatest, healing miracle, your immune system. So it destroys the invaders that cause your nasal and sinus discomfort. The world, respected, Nobel Prize Organization says it best. They reveal that your immune system stands guard and that any invader "will most likely be wiped out before there are any symptoms."

You cut your finger and it heals. You break a bone and it grows back together. Your body is an extraordinary, self-healing machine with amazingly, recuperative powers that far exceed the most effective drug ever invented.

The use of Flora Sinus is a natural healing method. Healing miracles are not the result of gulping down man-made drugs. Miracles of nature have evolved over millions of years. Modern medicine is a pale imitation of it.

A functioning, healthy immune system is an important step in ending your nasal and sinus problem and enjoying permanent relief.

THIRTY-SIX

BULLFIGHTERS

Bull fighting is an activity that has existed for many generations. Bull fighting is popular in Spain and Portugal. Bullfighters are trained to perform in large arenas. They wear a special outfit. They are called matadors.

Matadors must use a red cape to attract the attention of the bull. The matador comes into the arena before a large crowd of people. He wears a matador's hat, tight pants, special shoes and carries a red cape into the arena.

A matador has to be prepared to confront a large, angry bull. He charges at the bull. He flashes his red cape at the bull again and again. The bull rushes toward the red cape over and over because it reacts to the color red, which is a bright color.

Finally, the matador charges at the bull with a sword and stabs at the bull. The matador finally stabs the bull enough to kill it. The bull falls to the ground and dies. The matador is victorious. He wins and he is cheered by the large crowd. He leaves the arena with victory.

Matadors perform in big arenas regularly. They become famous as brave matadors. Bull fighting is a dangerous sport. Not everyone can become a matador. It takes courage, bravery and determination to become a matador.

THIRTY-SEVEN

ITALIAN ESCAPADE

Italy is a fascinating country in Southern Europe. It is shaped like a big boot. There are many scenic views of valleys, hillsides, olive trees, vineyards and farming areas. The ocean borders are in Southern Italy.

Italy is an enchanting country where tourists can escape from maddening crowds. Italy has many mysterious, intriguing places. Some delightful cities in Italy are Rome, Milan, Pisa and Florence.

Rome is the capital city in Italy. There are many, marvelous places to go to in Rome. The Fountain of Tivoli is a magnificent view of many fountains flowing down along one, lengthy wall. Visitors can observe the beautiful waterfalls and they can relax and escape from the bustle of city noises.

Roman Catholic cathedrals are very special places to seek peace and harmony. Sacred prayers are said to raise sacred vibrations. Latin chants are sacred. Church music creates a peaceful sound so anyone can feel better when they enter the cathedrals. There are cathedrals throughout Italy.

Rome has many balconies with spectacular views. You can sit in a chair and spend a lot of time looking at changing colors in the sky and at different, scenic views. The climate is generally very warm.

Roman ruins can easily be seen near the old section of Rome. The ground has sunk in the old section of this city. The newer part of the city is on a higher level. The new Rome is modern looking.

Many tourists come to Rome because Rome is a well known city in Italy. Roman temples can be seen in Rome. They are marvelous and very enormous. Roman temples have massive columns and pillars. Statues are on the Roman temples. These statues are situated around the temples.

Milan has many shops and plazas. There are outdoor gardens and tiled roof homes. Homes are made of clay and granite. Heavy stones are placed around the homes. There are magnificent patios, restaurants, shops and gardens.

Pisa is another Italian city. The famous, leaning Tower of Pisa stands high on a slant in Pisa. It began to lean gradually because of the foundation, which was unstable. Tourists were allowed to go in the Leaning Tower of Pisa until several decades ago. There is an excellent view of Pisa in the tower.

Florence is a religious city. Michelangelo painted the Sistine Chapel in this splendid city. Florentine artifacts are very artistic. Mosaics, vases, fountains, frescoes and carved stones are in Florence. This city is one of the most beautiful cities in the world.

You can escape to Italy to enjoy many, scenic views of trees, flowers, waterways, unique, Italian architecture and more. Your adventures are worth remembering.

THIRTY-EIGHT

ROMEO AND JULIET

<u>Romeo and Juliet</u> is a famous Shakespeare play. Shakespeare wrote many stage plays. <u>Romeo and Juliet</u> is one of Shakespeare's best plays. It is a romantic play about a young man and a young woman who fell in love. They were of different classes.

Romeo met Juliet during a social occasion. He danced with Juliet. He was attracted to her. She was attracted to Romeo. They decided to meet secretly. They didn't want their parents to find out that they had fallen in love.

Romeo secretly married Juliet. In time, Juliet's parents found out about Romeo. They strongly disapproved of Romeo pursuing their daughter Juliet.

Juliet's father wanted his daughter to marry a man that he had chosen for her. He had chosen a wealthy man.

Juliet did not want to marry the man her father had chosen for her. Romeo fought with his rivals who disapproved of his relationship with Juliet. She was told that she must marry in her own social class.

Juliet was told that Romeo was killed. She was very sad when she was told that he was not living. Juliet decided to drink some poison. She fell asleep. Romeo searched for Juliet. He found her in a burial area in a church. He was told she was poisoned. He thought she was dead.

As a result Romeo decided to drink some poison so he could die. He was beside Juliet. Juliet woke up. She saw Romeo at her side. She tried to wake him up. Romeo was dead. Juliet became very remorseful because Romeo was dead. In deep despair she decided to stab herself. She died at Romeo's side.

This tragic ending of the lives of Romeo and Juliet is a reminder of the injustice of class discrimination. Romeo and Juliet would have been happy in the 21st century. However, there has been class discrimination even one hundred years ago.

Social attitudes have changed generation after generation. More and more people have become open minded. More people accept a better way of life. Intermarriage between races is accepted today. More couples marry even if one of them is financially poor. Today people accept each other despite age, race, nationality and social class.

THIRTY-NINE

SHAKESPEARE PERSONIFIED

William Shakespeare was born in Stratford-upon-Avon in England in Great Britain. He decided to write stage plays when he grew up. He was an actor on the stage as well.

Shakespeare may have been Francis Bacon. Some people believe he was Francis Bacon who was related to Queen Elizabeth I. In any case Shakespeare grew up in a cultural environment. He spoke elegantly. He mastered the English language.

Shakespeare married Anne Hathaway during his early manhood. He lived in a cottage with his wife. He had three children. Shakespeare was not happy in his marriage. He met a woman who came from a higher class. He had a romantic relationship with her.

London, England was a larger city where cultural events took place. Shakespeare decided to move to London to perform on the London stage. He continued to write stage plays. He wrote over 35 stage plays. All of his stage plays were produced on the London stage and many of his plays were performed in Stratford-upon-Avon at the Shakespeare Playhouse.

William Shakespeare wrote poetic dialogue. His characters I his many plays had problems to face. Shakespeare wrote tragedies, comedies and he even wrote poetry. In <u>Hamlet</u> the ghost of Hamlet's father appeared before Hamlet. Hamlet's father communicated to his son. He hold Hamlet that he was murdered. Hamlet was upset to find out that his father was murdered.

Hamlet decided to avenge his father's death by finding the person who murdered his father, who had been the king before he was murdered. Shakespeare expressed strong feelings in his characters in the action and dialogue. He wrote many story plots with turning points and climaxes.

Many people in England came to see Shakespeare's plays. His plays were performed in open theaters. The audience sat in bench seats around the central theater. Audiences were allowed to respond orally about the behavior of the characters in Shakespeare's plays.

Shakespeare continued to write plays day and night. He also directed many of his original plays. Romeo and Juliet was based on Shakespeare's experience with a higher class lady. He had fallen in love with a beautiful, well-to-do lady. She came to see Shakespeare's plays. She even performed in some of his plays. William Shakespeare became famous because of his well written plays which were performed often in England.

William Shakespeare's plays have been performed around Europe and in North America. His plays are performed in Australia and Canada. His plays are considered to be classics. Shakespeare's plays are studied in high school and in college because they are treasured as English classics.

Some of Shakespeare's well known plays are <u>Hamlet</u>, <u>Othello</u>, <u>As You Like It</u>, <u>King Lear</u>, <u>King Richard III</u>, <u>Romeo and Juliet</u> and more.

CHAPTER FORTY

FAMOUS ARTISTS

Becoming an artist is a creative experience. Many artists have existed in the world. One of the most well known artists was Michelangelo.

Michelangelo grew up in Italy in a small town. He began learning to carve granite and clay when he was a young man. He moved to Florence in Italy and continued creating sculptures. He became known for sculptures of Mother Mary and Jesus and King David of Israel.

Michelangelo was asked to paint the Sistine Chapel. He painted the hands of Godly Hosts touching fingers in the heavens. He painted the entire ceiling in the Sistine Chapel.

Michelangelo was asked to build St. John's Cathedral in Vatican City. He designed and built St. John's Cathedral. St. John's Cathedral is the largest Catholic Church in the world. Millions of people visit Vatican City every year. They go into St. John's Cathedral to observe this magnificent, church structure.

Vincent Van Gogh was an unusual artist. He experimented with bright colors. He painted countryside scenes, household objects and self portraits. He painted portraits of other people. He painted women cooking in the kitchen, churches, homes and ocean scenes. Van Gogh was a unique painter. Bright colors made a difference in his paintings.

Vincent Van Gogh's paintings were displayed in art galleries by his brother. Many people came to the art galleries in Holland. They appreciated Vincent Van Gogh's paintings. His brother took his paintings to be displayed in art museums in Holland. Eventually his paintings were sent to other art museums. Van Gogh's paintings became well known.

Paul Gauguin painted pictures of Polynesian women in French Polynesia. His paintings became well known. Renoir was a painter of gardens and lily ponds. His vivid colors added to each painting. His famous paintings express a feeling of serenity and quiet beauty.

Rubens became well known for his portraits of Dutch people. He painted the way they dressed in the 1800s. Rubens was accurate in his description of people.

Rembrandt became known for using lower class individuals painted in upper class costumes. He painted average, looking people as important, Dutch noblemen. He painted very large paintings of life-size people.

Pablo Picasso became famous for painting surrealistic scenes. His pictures had perverted drawings. Yet, he became well known for developing a different, art style.

Diego Rivera is famous in South America and Mexico for his descriptive scenes in Mexico and South America. He painted large, scenic views with Latin American people in many of his paintings. His art work has become well known.

Famous artists are recognized for their unique style of art. They have contributed to a new form of art which is recognized and appreciated around the world.

FORTY-ONE

FILMMAKING

Filmmaking began in the 1920s in Hollywood, California. MGM Studios, Fox Studios, Paramount Studios and other movie studios developed films. Movies began in black and white. The first movies had no sound.

Captions were used under the silent film to reveal the dialogue. Each film that was produced required skills in how to film each scene. Film photographers have been trained to film each scene in the films they help create.

Film photographers produce close-up scenes and far away scenes. By the late 1920s films were made in color. By the 1930s sound was added to films. Many filmmakers continued to produce black and white films.

Eventually films were produced mostly in color. Sound tracks were produced in all films. Sound effects and dialogue spoken by actors and actresses added to the emotional effect in the films.

Many films have been filmed in each decade. Well known stars have performed in different movies. Some well known movie stars are Carole Lombard, Dick Powell, William Powell, Marian Davies, James Stewart, Betty Grable, Jean Harlow, Rita Hayworth, Hedy Lamour, Robert Taylor, Spencer Tracy, Stewart Granger, Charleton Heston, Jean Simmons, Elizabeth Taylor, Clark Gable and more.

Filmmakers move cameras on platforms in order to film moving objects and people running and walking around. The way a film is spliced and put together scene by scene makes a difference in how it turns out.

Thousands of films have been produced from the 1920s through 2008. Many types of films have been produced. There are travelogues, human interest films, family dramas, science topics, archaeology and history, soap operas and romance dramas, etc.

Filmmaking is versatile and popular. More and more people are learning to produce films. A person can learn a lot about the film industry. More people study filmmaking in college. They are able to earn a B.A. in filmmaking. More creative people are learning to produce interesting films.

FORTY-TWO

TALK SHOWS

Talk shows are popular on television. The purpose for talk shows is so people can interact in order to talk about important issues and topics. Talk shows have been presented on television for many years.

The Tonight Show was a popular talk show in the 1960s, 1970s and 1980s. Johnny Carson was the host of The Tonight Show. Comedy scenes were presented on The Tonight Show. Johnny Carson presented jokes. He dressed in many, funny costumes. He wore funny hats. The Tonight Show was on television for many years.

The Andy Williams Show was a variety of vocal music performances. Andy Williams was the host.

He sang many tenor solos. His show was popular for years.

The Dinah Shore Show became popular. Dinah Shore was the host of her show. She sang many vocal solos. She wore beautiful clothes on her show.

Steve Allen was a talk show host. He presented jokes and stories. He performed in skits on his show. Talk shows continue to be presented on television. The hosts continue to change. Yet the techniques of presenting a talk show continue to be presented. Significant issues and topics are still presented.

FORTY-THREE

DOMESTICATED PEOPLE

Domesticated people are people who generally like to stay home. They spend much of their time in their homes. They dwell indoors and in their gardens. So, they decorate their homes to meet their need for comfort, beauty and privacy.

Living at home is a domestic experience. How people decorate their homes affects the way they are living. Our home is important to us because we need a place to relax and retreat from the outside world. Most people expect to be able to go home to a safe, comfortable place to live.

Domesticated people take care of their residence. They take pride in where they live. They know how to select a home in an appropriate neighborhood. Because domestic people usually spend more time at home they want to be surrounded by responsible neighbors. They have more of an opportunity to meet their neighbors. The more they know their neighbors and surrounding environment the more secure they feel.

Domesticated people tend to stay home a lot. Their home is their retreat. A homebody person surrounds herself or himself with artistic displays such as beautiful paintings, artifacts, knick knacks, plants, useful and comfortable furnishings. Such people select colorful, interesting carpets and many, household items.

Domesticated people tend to eat most of their meals at home. They have learned to cook many delicious meals to nourish themselves. They would rather eat home cooked meals than to eat out at restaurants. They have become used to eating at home.

Domestic endeavors are important to people who stay home. Housework and regular cleaning is important. A clean home is a healthy place to live. Domestic people know how to vacuum carpets, dust furniture, sweep floors, wash windows, wash and dry dishes, wash clothes, iron clothes, make beds, clean sinks and toilets. They learn how to mow lawns, weed gardens and water their yards.

It is worth being a domestic person. One's home is an important place to dwell in and appreciate the lovely atmosphere one has created.

FORTY-FOUR

AMERICAN PRESIDENTIAL
DEBATES IN 2008

American presidential debates take place before every American presidential election. The purpose for political debates is to have presidential candidates express their viewpoints, opinions and policies which they plan to use if they become the President of the United States of America.

Barack Obama is the Democratic candidate running in 2008. John McCain is the Republican candidate running in 2008. The first debate was on September 15, 2008. The second debate was on October 15, 2008. The debaters were interviewed by a moderator on television.

A series of questions were asked by moderators who interviewed Barack Obama and John McCain. During the first debate the following questions were asked. The moderator asked, "What would you do if there was another 9-11 crisis?" John McCain replied, "I plan to go after Osama Bin Laden and the Al-Qaida movement. I will have them captured and killed. I will wait until Iraq is safe and the Iraqis have maintained democracy."

The debate moderator asked Barack Obama the same question. Barack Obama said, "I will go after Osama Bin Laden and have him killed." The moderator said, "You both agree on this issue." The moderator continued by asking, "How will you handle the American economy?" Barack Obama answered first. He said, "I will lower taxes for 95% of Americans who earn less than $250,000,00 a year. I will raise taxes for Americans who earn more than $250,000.00."

John McCain answered this question in the following manner. He said, "I will not raise taxes for the wealthy Americans. They have a right to keep their income without more taxes."

The moderator asked, "How will you handle the problems with Iran?" Barack Obama replied, "I am willing to communicate with the Iran leaders. George Bush has not had communications with the Iran leaders. He refuses to speak to President Jad." John McCain said with strong feelings, "I will not speak to President Jad without pre-conditions. President Jad said, 'I will make corpse out of the Israelites!' "Under these conditions I will not speak to him," John McCain said.

The moderator asked, "What healthcare programs do you endorse?" John McCain said, "Too much money is spent for Medicare. I will give $5,000.00 to each person for health insurance." Barack Obama said, "I will provide health benefits for all Americans. I will protect Medicare for the Middle Class." Barack Obama said, "A person has a right to choose her own doctor. He or she can choose a specific, medical plan to meet the person's needs."

Barack Obama continued by saying, "We need change in America. John McCain has voted 90% for Bush policies. George Bush policies have failed. The Middle Class needs economic changes. They need affordable, health insurance."

Barack Obama won the first presidential debate. During the second presidential debate Barack Obama continued to talk about the need for changes in the economy, healthcare and the war in Iraq.

John McCain believes he has already been tested. He is a war hero because he served in the Viet Nam War. He suffered in a Viet Nam prison for five and a half years. He tried to remain brave and he raised the morale of American prisoners.

Barack Obama was ahead in the presidential race by ten percent. Many Americans want positive changes in America. Eight years of the Bush administration has caused our economy to fall. The war in Iraq has been going on for nearly six years. It costs $10 billion a month for the war to continue. Barack Obama said, "We need to go after Al-Qaida in Pakistan in order to stop the war."

Many people believe the war in Iraq should end. Our American economy has been badly affected in the last eight years. We are $10 trillion in debt in America. Barack Obama has said he will pay the American debt within eight years.

Barack Obama stated that other methods of fuel should be created. He focused on solar, electric, wind and natural fuels which should be used. He said, "We should not have to rely on the Middle East for oil. We should become independent from other nations and countries for fuel. Natural fuels stop air pollution."

Barack Obama wants to improve the education system in America. He believes in early, childhood education. He wants young children to have a quality education. The election takes place on Tuesday, November 4, 2008. Everyone should go out and vote.

Ralph Nader was the presidential candidate for the Freedom Party. He had progressive policies to help change America's economy, environment, healthcare and foreign policies. He believed the war in Iraq should end as soon as possible. Nader wanted to change the Federal Government because he believes the American Federal Government of America has been corrupted. The American Federal Government should not be able to collect taxes and to control the American economy. Nader believes in preserving the American environment.

Natural gas can be used. Green gases are not healthy to breathe into our lungs. The present medical insurance in America is controlled by the insurance companies. Their prices are way too high. Elderly people generally cannot afford healthcare benefits if they are on a limited income. Many Americans are unable to choose healthcare benefits. This is unfair.

Baldwin is the presidential candidate for the Independent Party. He believes the Federal Government should not control American money. He believes a new money system should be developed which protects the American people. Corrupt, wealthy businessmen have controlled Wall Street Stock Market. The Wall Street Stock Market has nearly crashed. The cost of houses has gone up because of greed. Americans have been losing their homes because of the high costs they pay to mortgage companies and American banks. There should be housing regulations according to Baldwin.

Cynthia McKinney is the presidential candidate for the Green Party. She has stated that Americans should have a strong voice in the economy, about the natural environment and there should be ethical, voting rights. The voting machines should not be rigged. She believes electrical cars should be used in place of gasoline and oil fueled cars and other vehicles.

Each presidential candidate has developed policies about major issues and needs in America. Each presidential candidate has the opportunity to make positive changes needed in America.

Barack Obama won the November 4, 2008 Presidential election with 333 electoral votes. John McCain received 157 electoral votes. Barack Obama will be inaugurated as the 44th American President on January 20, 2009. His political strategy is to promote significant changes in governmental policies to meet the needs of the American people. Many people think Barack Obama will make an excellent President of the U.S.A.

FORTY-FIVE

TELEVISION BROADCAST
NEWS REPORTERS

Television news reporters have a pertinent job presenting the news on television. They must dress in a professional manner. There are men and women newscasters.

A T.V. news reporter must speak clearly and look in the television camera with a professional approach. The daily news and nightly news must be presented with clarity and accuracy.

There are many topics and issues presented in the news. Different news channels are CNN News, BBC News, Fox News and local news. World news and some local news are presented every day.

Significant events, activities, factual information and announcements are presented on television news. The most current happenings are presented in the news. What, where, who, when and how are expressed in the news. The most important events and experiences are described. We learn about what happens in the world and in our local area when we listen to the news regularly.

T.V. news reporters are given daily news scripts to read while they are presenting the news on television. They look into the television camera in order to get the attention of the television audience. They are presenting the news to millions of people. They must be understood and heard so the news is received and comprehended.

Many T.V. news reporters have presented the news on television. They have a variety of new topics so the audience will stay interested in the news.

T.V. news reporters are needed around the world. Sometimes news is sad. Other times news is cheerful. All the essential news is presented whether it is alarming, depressing or cheerful news. People broaden their awareness of world events, issues and happenings by watching television news.

FORTY-SIX

METAPHYSICAL BOOKS

Metaphysical books have been published since 1875 on in America. Metaphysical books are about invisible realities that exist on other planes. Ancient wisdom and knowledge are stated in different, metaphysical books.

Madame Helena Blavatsky wrote metaphysical books such as Isis Unveiled, The Secret Doctrine, Keys to Theosophy and news pamphlets about Theosophy and Metaphysics.

Francia La Due, the first Guardian-in-Chief of The Temple of the People, wrote messages given by Master Hilarion, which were published in The Temple Teachings in Volumes One, Two and Three.

William Quan Judge, co-founder of The Theosophical Society, wrote pamphlets about Theosophy and Metaphysical truths. William David Dower, second Guardian-in-Chief wrote <u>Oceans of Theosophy</u> and lesson booklets about Temple teachings entitled <u>Occultism for Beginners</u> and <u>The Heart Doctrine</u>. He wrote <u>Yellow and Red Folios</u> about messages of metaphysical truths and teachings given by Master Morya, Masters Hilarion and Kuthumi.

Manley Hall, who was a knowledgeable adept, wrote many books about Occultism and Metaphysics. He became well known in Southern California.

The St. Germain Foundation, which has been established in America in the 1930s, is a metaphysical, esoteric group. Books have been written by the religious leader, Guy Ballard. He wrote <u>The Magic Presence</u>, <u>Unveiled Mysteries</u> and <u>St. Germain Decree Books</u>.

The Summit Lighthouse established by Mark Prophet in 1958 is a New Age Metaphysical group. Many metaphysical books have been published such as <u>Climb the Highest Mountain</u>, <u>St. Germain on Alchemy</u>, <u>Mysteries of the Holy Grail</u> and <u>Lost Years of Jesus</u>.

More metaphysical groups have been established around the world. More and more metaphysical books are being written. White Eagle is another messenger. Ruth Montgomery has written <u>The World Before</u> and <u>The World Beyond</u>. Cecelia Frances Page has written <u>Awaken To Spiritual Illumination</u> and <u>Mystical Realities</u>. You can order Cecelia Frances Page's books at <u>www.iUniverse.com</u>. Dr. Goldberg, a hypnotherapist wrote <u>Past Lives, Future Lives</u> and <u>Time Travelers from the Future</u>.

You can purchase metaphysical books at metaphysical, religious foundations mentioned in this article. You can order some books from local bookstores. You have an opportunity to learn about metaphysical truths.

FORTY-SEVEN

CHERYL'S HITCHHIKING EXPERIENCES

Hitchhiking is a common practice. People without cars, who are broke, usually try to hitchhike. A hitchhiker stands near a road, street or highway. He or she puts up his or her thumb to let passersby know they need a ride.

Hitchhiking is risky. Drivers who stop to pick up hitchhikers are taking a chance as well. Some hitchhikers are trustworthy and pleasant. Other hitchhikers may cause problems and even become dangerous. Some hitchhikers depend on different drivers to provide transportation across many miles.

Hitchhikers learn about many people while they travel across the country. They are given the opportunity to have conversations with the driver and anyone else already in a car, truck, van or bus. Hitchhikers sit where they are asked to sit in a vehicle.

Young girls and attractive, young women should be careful if they decide to hitchhike. They could be raped, robbed and injured.

Cheryl Tedford, who was 22 years old, became a hitchhiker because she was unemployed and she didn't have a car. She was homeless and broke. She frequently walked everywhere because she kept moving around. She wore blue jeans and a warm pullover sweater. She also wore a jacket when it was cold outside. She wore a pair of leather boots that were sturdy.

Cheryl was courageous and fearless when she traveled by foot and when she hitchhiked. She had faith that each person who picked her up in their vehicle could be trusted. She avoided having young men in their late teens and twenties pick her up in order to protect herself from being raped and molested. She accepted transportation from couples, women and older men.

Hitchhiking became a way of traveling for Cheryl Tedford for years to come. She worked part-time here and there to pay for food. She was too young to receive Social Security benefits. The money she earned was money she kept on her in a money belt. She hid her money to protect it.

Cheryl bought raw fruit and vegetables which she carried in her backpack. She kept several blankets, a toothbrush and toothpaste, a comb and hairbrush in her backpack. She had an extra set of clothing for travel purposes.

When it rained and snowed Cheryl stayed in old barns or old, rundown houses which were uninhabited. She stayed overnight often in rundown places to keep the rain, sleet and snow off of her.

Cheryl was strong, healthy and enthusiastic about life and she kept meeting more and more people. She was inquisitive and bright. Cheryl had good eyesight and hearing. She was not glamorous or especially pretty. She was rather plain. This did not bother her. She lived a simple life.

Hitchhiking was an educational experience. She wore a wristwatch so she could keep track of the time. She sometimes risked her life by traveling at night. She sometimes walked for many hours during the day when she didn't hitchhike.

Cheryl enjoyed visiting with people she traveled with. They often asked her where she was going. They asked why she hitchhiked in order to travel. Cheryl explained that she was unemployed and couldn't afford to have her own car.

In five years Cheryl managed to travel all over the United States of America. She went through every state on the mainland of America. She was unharmed when she walked and hitchhiked.

Cheryl's philosophy of life was based on freedom of choice, freedom of speech and freedom of religious beliefs. She listened to many people during her journeys around America. She was a free thinker and she was an independent person.

In time Cheryl became employed full time in a public library. She was able to read many library books which she selected to read. She learned a lot about ideas, descriptions of life, people and places. She used her imagination. She began writing in a journal about her hitchhiking experiences and travels. She described many scenic places and interesting people.

Cheryl remained a free spirit throughout her life. She continued to enjoy traveling, reading, writing and searching for universal truths.

FORTY-EIGHT

PEACEFUL MOMENTS

Peaceful moments help us experience harmony, love and inner balance. White light descends down into the soul presence and four lower bodies known as mental, emotional, physical and astral forms.

Every peaceful moment awakens the soul and mind to God reality. White light carries the pure consciousness of God into our souls and minds. We receive a clearer vision of truth, purity, wisdom and God consciousness.

Peaceful moments remind us of who we really are. When we merge our minds and spirit with God we become one with all life because we experience true peace, love, harmony, serenity and awareness.

We have the opportunity to become close to nature and cosmic reality. Our peace of mind is sent out into the world. When we maintain peace of mind we are helping ourselves and others to experience peaceful co-existence.

FORTY-NINE

SKETCHINGS

Sketchings are drawings produced with graphite pencils and colored pencils in sketch pads. Artists often draw sketches which they develop more thoroughly. The sketches can remain black and white. Most likely the best sketches are filled in with oil paints or water color paints. They become paintings and they no longer look like sketchings.

Cartoonists develop pencil sketches of cartoon figures which are described in regular cartoons in funny, cartoon books and in newspaper cartoons.

Sketches may remain untouched and displayed in art galleries. Sketchings reveal details in pencil designs.

Pencil designs sometimes reveal visual creations more clearly in a basic way.

Many beginning artists learn to sketch on art paper so they learn to outline the scene they are describing. They can finish a sketch faster than a painting. Sketches usually are easier to complete. Many sketches are black and white.

Famous sketches have been created by Grandma Moses, an elderly lady who became an artist late in life. She has sketched hundreds of artistic sketches. Grandma Moses has become well known for many original sketches. Many of her sketches have been sold to different people.

It is worthwhile learning to draw and to sketch. Portraits can be sketched at art shows in parks, at Disneyland and at County Fairs. Enjoy learning to sketch a variety of scenes.

FIFTY

FAMILY PHOTOS

Most families have family photos which are usually kept in photo albums. The family, photo albums have many photographs of different, family members.

Grandparents, great-grandparents, nieces, nephews, cousins, aunts, uncles, brothers and sisters, mothers and fathers are in photographs. The photos are generally organized throughout the photo album.

It is enjoyable to look through family, photo albums. Photos bring back fond memories of different stages in our lives. For instance, our parents usually take photos regularly of different babyhood, toddler, childhood, teen years and adulthood stages for each of their children. Many memories are recalled when we review family photos.

Family photos are taken at family reunions, picnics, beach parties, church functions, birthday parties, weddings and many, other occasions. Each photo brings back memories of what family members did at different events and celebrations.

During family reunions and during holidays such as Christmas, Thanksgiving, at birthday parties and slumber parties, etc, family photos can be enjoyed. Family photos are an historic proof of what family members have experienced and how they look throughout time.

Family albums should be treasured by one's family. Family albums should be kept in dry, safe places. Photos should be covered with clear, plastic covers and sealed off from moisture, heat and dust. Photographs can last a long time if they are protected and carefully preserved.

Some photographs are black and white. Other photos are in color. Colorful photographs are very interesting to enjoy looking at. Color is preserved in photos that are protected and stored away carefully. Photos help us appreciate the past. There are photos of vivid scenery as well as of people we know. We can collect photos of friends, classmates and other people.

FIFTY-ONE

HOUSEKEEPERS AND MAIDS

Housekeepers have learned to clean different houses. Some houses are very large. Some houses are relatively small. A good housekeeper knows how to vacuum carpets, dust furniture properly, mop floors and sweep floors, porches and decks.

Housekeepers clear out spider webs and dust in every room. They know how to clean windows, skylights and high windows in a house. Cleaning chandeliers is another challenge. Each part of a chandelier must be polished after the parts are dusted carefully.

Housekeepers know how to take care of houses. They learn how to clean toilets, sinks and bathtubs by using cleaning methods and scrubbing substances.

Bathroom facilities and kitchens can be kept spotless if properly cleaned.

Generally housekeepers are paid minimum wages up to $20.00 an hour. They establish clients and work out time schedules to clean houses and apartments. Usually cleaning equipment is available at each house or apartment. Housekeepers are paid by the job for each household.

A maid service company usually exists in each large town or community. Maids are hired at the maid service company when clients call in to hire maids.

Housekeepers are needed on a regular basis. Many households need professional housecleaning. Hotel managers and motel managers hire maids to clean hotel and motel rooms. Maids must sweep, dust and straighten out rooms. They change beds and put on clean sheets and pillowcases. Clean, fresh towels and wash rags are put in the hotel and motel rooms. Old towels, wash rags and old sheets and pillowcases are taken out of each hotel and motel room and placed in a dispenser basket.

Hotels and motels must be cleaned each day so the rooms can be ready for new customers. Sanitation and cleanliness are required to maintain every hotel and motel.

FIFTY-TWO

HOW TO SLEEP WELL

It is important to sleep well. You need a quiet time to restore your body each night. Before going to bed you should clear your mind of emotional, negative thoughts. Drink a cup of chamomile tea or a glass of warm milk.

Be sure your mattress is comfortable. Warm blankets and clean sheets and pillowcases help you feel better when you lie down to sleep. Say some prayers before you go to sleep.

If your mind is filled with strong, emotional feelings about something you are concerned about, it usually takes longer to fall asleep. You need to relax so your mind calms down. You will go to sleep much faster because you are relaxed.

Your mind is always conscious even when you sleep. Many people dream once they go to sleep because their minds are conscious in the dream state. Some people remember their most vivid dreams. Dreams usually reflect some memories and associates with one's experiences on Earth. Sometimes dreams are caused by subconscious thoughts stored in one's subconscious mind.

Generally people who sleep well at night are able to feel better the next day. When a person receives enough rest he or she can function much better the next day. A good night's sleep is important to maintain good health.

Sometimes we wake up in the middle of the night because we have to go to the bathroom. When we go back to bed we are still wide awake. It takes time to go back to sleep. We need to relax our minds so we can drift back to sleep. Once we fall asleep again we generally are able to rest and receive the sleep we need so we can face the next day.

Strength and vitality rejuvenate our bodies from getting enough rest. So, learn to relax and calm your mind and body so you can sleep better.

FIFTY-THREE

FACING UP TO CHALLENGES

Challenges occur regularly in everyone's life. How do we face up to challenges? Each person must learn to cope with challenges and unexpected events.

Something may be a challenge to one person. Yet this so-called challenge may not be a challenge to someone else. For example, having teeth pulled may cause someone a lot of pain. Another person may respond in a more relaxed manner while his or her teeth are being pulled out.

A person may fall and break a leg. The pain is exasperating while the leg is broken. The leg may have to be reset so it can heal. The leg is usually covered with a cast. Crutches will have to be used until a person can walk again. Once the leg is healed then the person needs to use a cane for a while. One person accepts the broken leg and endures pain until he or she is well. Another person is in sheer agony and has a lot of difficulty accepting the broken leg.

Attitudes make a difference in how people accept challenges. One person may face challenges optimistically. Another person falls apart and does not cope well regarding the same type of challenges. Each person is an individual. Each person has different values and beliefs.

The more positive, accepting and forgiving a person is the more easily he or she faces difficulties in life. Positive people tend to be more successful and cooperative. They are more open and feel freer to make wise decisions. Every problem can be overcome as well as faced.

Challenges make us stronger. When we face each challenge we have learned to accept and face adversity and difficulties with maturity.

FIFTY-FOUR

DOLL MAKERS

Dolls have been created for many centuries. Doll makers have learned to produce creative,doll patterns. The arms and legs of a doll must fit the body of each doll. Some dolls are made of plastic. Other dolls are made of rubber or porcelain. The hair is sewn onto a doll's head. The hair may be black, brown, red or blonde.

Doll's hair must be curled and hair may be straight. Eyelashes need to be sewn onto the eyelashes. Eyebrows need to be sewn into the forehead above the two eyes of each doll.

Most dolls are made in doll factories. Sometimes the hair and eyelashes are sewn by machine. Each doll may have a different hairstyle. Once the dolls are produced they are matched with certain clothes and doll's shoes. Shiny shoes look good. Some doll's shoes have straps. Other shoes have shoe laces or buckles.

Some dolls are dressed in fancy clothes. Other dolls have on casual clothes. Children usually want dolls. Parents buy dolls for their children.

Doll makers produce different dolls with different colored bodies. Some dolls are white. Others are black or yellow. Different races are depicted when dolls are made. Black children usually play with black dolls. Chinese and Japanese children play with yellow dolls. White dolls are played with by white children. Frizzy hair is produced on black dolls.

Doll factories exist around the world in different countries. Europeans make a lot of dolls. Some dolls are soldiers, princesses, pixies, elflike, porcelain dwarfs and regular boy and girl dolls. Dolls of the world are dressed in their native costumes.

Dolls are displayed in shelves and arranged around different parts of the house. Many dolls are sold in stores for children to enjoy. Adults enjoy dolls as well to collect as a hobby.

FIFTY-FIVE

THE EXCEPTIONAL TEACHER

Exceptional teachers are generally rare. An exceptional teacher excels beyond what is expected from teachers. These outstanding teachers are highly organized with specific goals and purposes. Outstanding teachers decorate their classrooms with interesting, colorful, bulletin boards. They display artifacts and other, visual objects for their students to enjoy.

Exceptional teachers truly educate their students. They provide enrichment and knowledge worth learning about. These outstanding educators are respected by their students. Students appreciate having outstanding teachers who inspire and encourage them to excel in school. The learning process becomes exciting and really worthwhile.

Serena Halstead decided to become a high school Social Studies and History teacher. She received a B.S. degree in Social Studies and History when she was 24 years old. Serena was enthusiastic about teaching. She found a teaching position in her home town starting in the fall.

When school started Serena prepared her classroom with colorful, educational bulletin boards about History and Social Studies topics. She used a variety of visual materials so that every bulletin board would be dynamic and meaningful.

Serena prepared her lesson plans for Social Studies and History. She was assigned three, Social Studies classes and two, History classes. She wrote neatly and carefully in her lesson plan book. Her Social Studies lesson plans were written in one section. Her History lesson plans were written in another section.

The lesson plans were organized with objectives, specific listed books and page numbers for each lesson. Serena kept the lesson plan book on her desk. Assignments were listed for each school day. Serena, who was called Ms. Halstead, went to teacher meetings and workshops. She was more prepared to teach. She met other teachers at her high school who she shared educational concepts and objectives with.

Preparation for classes was on Monday and Tuesday. Students returned to school on Wednesday. Serena observed her first class of students walk into her classroom and sit down. The school bell rang. Serena introduced herself. She stood before the class and said, "I am Ms. Halstead. I am your Social Studies teacher this year. I want all of you to ask questions and make worthwhile comments. If you think about what you are learning during class time and when you read in the textbooks and other books you will absorb knowledge."

The students looked at Serena with surprised expressions. Few teachers spoke this way to them. Stella, one of the students, asked, "Is this our Social Studies textbook?" Stella held up her textbook. Serena replied, "Yes. Notice the title of your textbook. Please read the title aloud."

Stella read orally, "Current Social Issues and Problems in the World." Tony, another student, commented, "This is some title!" Ms. Halstead said,

"Have you noticed who the author is?" Stella replied with excitement, "You are the author, Ms. Halstead."

Serena Halstead smiled and commented, "Yes. I wrote this book several years ago. It was published last year. Please open your book to Chapter One. We will read orally and then we will discuss the problems and issues." Ms. Halstead called on Larry Henderson to read orally.

Larry Henderson began reading orally. He read, "Current world problems and major world crises are caused because leaders have not found better ways to resolve problems. Each world crisis can be solved step by step. It takes insight and wise decisions to resolve each problem."

Ms. Halstead asked her students, "How would you resolve world crises such as war, poverty and diseases?" The class sat in their chairs trying to think of answers. Senora, another student, replied, "Leaders should be able to agree about ways to solve their differences about certain problems and issues."

Ms. Halstead responded, "That is a good comment Senora. Think of specific ways a war can be stopped without violence." Senora responded, "Effective communications can help leaders to understand how to agree on peaceful ways to clear up pertinent issues and problems."

Ms. Halstead stood before her Social Studies class and said, "I want you to list ways to promote peace and to stop bloodshed." The class took out paper and pencils. They wrote down ways to promote peace.

Students were asked to share their solutions about promoting peace. They stated their ideas. Many students wrote many positive solutions to promote world peace.

Ms. Halstead collected the class statements. She reviewed their thoughts. She stimulated her students to keep thinking about realistic solutions to other major problems such as poverty, starvation and diseases. She was an exceptional teacher because she inspired her students to think and to become involved in finding ways to solve world problems and resolve world issues. Ms. Halstead asked her students to develop research projects about world crises and how to solve the crises. She stimulated her students to think for themselves.

FIFTY-SIX

FLIGHT TO PARADISE

Stanley and Harriet Jackson were ready for a vacation. They had been working hard on their jobs for years. They were due for a pleasant break. So they planned to take a flight to somewhere special. They were in their thirties and they lived in Cleveland, Ohio.

Harriet and Stanley went to talk to a travel agent near their home. The travel agent presented different, travel options. He handed them brochures to look at so they could make up their minds where they would travel to.

There were brochures about a variety of tropical islands such as Hawaii, Bermuda, the Bahamas, the Philippine Islands, Fiji, New Zealand and the Virgin

Islands. The Jacksons were overwhelmed with the many, possible selections.

Finally after reviewing all the travel brochures they decided to go to the Bahamian Islands for their vacation to relax and to enjoy themselves. The brochures had pictures of tropical, palm trees and magnificent, ocean scenes, beaches and resorts.

Harriet and Stanley were excited about traveling to some paradise resort. They made plans to go to the Bahamian Islands. Their flight to these islands was on Continental Airlines. They planned to stay in a resort hotel near the beach when they arrived in the islands.

The flight from the mainland would take ten hours. Once Harriet and Stanley boarded Continental Airlines they sat in first class. Their seats were comfortable and they had window views. There were some clouds in the sky when they left Cleveland, Ohio. The clouds were puffy and whitish-gray.

During the flight Harriet and Stanley were served an evening meal. They had a choice of baked chicken with rice and steamed vegetables or roast beef stroganoff with noodles and steamed vegetables. Harriet selected baked chicken and Stanley chose roast beef stroganoff. For dessert there was chocolate cake with a creamy filling. They were served tea or coffee. Harriet had lemon tea and Stanley had coffee.

After dinner the Jacksons relaxed and watched travelogues of different places on television. Then they fell asleep in the comfortable, recliner chairs. A stewardess covered them with warm blankets.

Stanley and Harriet arrived in the Bahamian Islands at Nassau on New Providence Island at 7:00 a.m. the next morning. They collected their belongings in the airport. Then they had breakfast in a restaurant at their resort hotel. They took a taxi to their hotel. Their luggage was taken to their plush, hotel room.

The hotel restaurant served a buffet breakfast. There was a wide variety of breakfast food. Harriet and Stanley selected omelets, hash brown potatoes, tropical fruit, mango tea, waffles and pancakes. Their breakfast was sumptuous.

The view from the restaurant was magnificent. Harriet and Stanley saw turquoise, blue colors in the ocean. Tropical birds were flying around outside the large, bay windows. They heard enchanting bird sounds. Tropical, palm trees were near the beach.

After breakfast Stanley and Harriet strolled on the beach near their hotel. The warm, beige, beach sand was easy to walk on. They walked over to the warm, ocean currents. The sand near the rolling ocean was wet.

Harriet and Stanley walked near the ocean on the wet sand. Ocean waves flowed over the sand onto their feet. There were interesting shells on the beach. They stopped to look at a variety of shells such as scallop shells, clam shells and some sand dollars.

Stanley and Harriet walked for several miles on the beach. They saw many shells. There was sea kelp which smelled of brine in the ocean. The ocean breeze was refreshing and pleasant. The breeze caressed their skin to cool them off. Palm trees swayed in the wind.

Stanley and Harriet decided to sit down under a shady, palm tree. They observed passersby and dogs roaming on the pristine beach. Ocean waves continued to move back and forth at the shore. Stanley and Harriet wanted to relax and rest after walking for several miles on the beach.

Finally it was time to head back to the hotel. As Harriet and Stanley were walking some wild dogs approached them. They were barking and yelping before they came close to Harriet and Stanley.

Stanley decided to pick up some rocks on the beach. He threw them swiftly at each wild dog to scare them away. The wild dogs yelped and ran away in the opposite direction. Harriet and Stanley were relieved that the dogs ran away.

The walk back to the hotel was warm. Fortunately Harriet and Stanley were wearing straw, sun hats. Once in a while the wind blew against their bodies. When they reached the hotel they went into their hotel room and took cool showers to cool off their skin.

It was time for lunch at midday. Stanley and Harriet decided to walk into the nearby village to select a restaurant to have their lunch. Stanley saw a Calypso restaurant. He told Harriet that he wanted to eat there. So the two of them walked into this restaurant.

The Calypso restaurant was decorated with tropical plants and island, art work and artifacts. A beautiful, flowing fountain was in the center of the room. There were miniature dolphins made of plaster in the fountain. Manmade mermaids were floating in the fountain.

Art work by Caribbean artists was displayed on the walls. A colorful carpet was covered on the floor. Dining tables were arranged around the large room. Colorful tablecloths were arranged on the tables. Beautiful, tropical flowers were arranged around the room.

A hostess greeted Stanley and Harriet at the entrance of the restaurant. She was dressed in a Calypso costume and she wore sandals. She had long, black hair and she was a Bahamian. She took the Jacksons to a table near the flowing fountain. Reggae music was heard. A Calypso band was performing with conga drums and guitars. Performers were singing Reggae music. The people in the Bahamas spoke with a British accent.

A waitress brought menus to Harriet and Stanley's table. They studied the menus carefully. Stanley and Harriet decided to have a fish dinner with brown rice and a medley of tropical vegetables. They were served papaya, shredded coconut and bananas for dessert. Their whole meal was very tasty and nutritious.

Harriet and Stanley listened to the Reggae performers. They had a wonderful time in this Calypso restaurant. However, the bill for the meal came to $68.00. They had mango tea at the end of the meal. Stanley and Harriet seldom spent that much money for one meal.

The Jacksons took a ferry ride over to a resort with a marble, pyramid building. There were Greek temples with marble columns. The modern architects made the buildings look like ancient Atlantis which existed there at one time. The outside of the buildings looked like Atlantean architecture.

Inside the building tourist restaurants, hotel accommodations and gambling casinos existed. There was a giant aquarium with tropical fish, coral and sea plants. Stanley and Harriet gazed into the aquarium with amazement and wonder.

The Jacksons flew over to Bimini Island north of New Providence in a small plane. They landed in an airfield in the woods. They took a taxi to a ferry near the ocean. They went to North Bimini Island. They checked into a hotel near the beach. Once they were settled in they decided to walk along the narrow, pristine sand. They were able to walk from the north to the south side of this island in a short period of time. The island was one-eighth of a mile in width. However, it was approximately forty miles long.

Once they returned to the hotel the Jacksons booked a diving tour to the Atlantean ruins. The Atlantean ruins were thirty to sixty feet under the ocean off the north coast of Bimini Island.

Harriet and Stanley put on scuba diving suits. They swam down with other scuba divers to the Atlantean ruins. They saw big, stone roads and large, stone walls. It looked like a harbor that sank into the ocean.

Scientists have stated that these Atlantean ruins were above water more than eleven thousand years ago. These ruins were discovered in 1968 by Manson Valentine, who is an archaeologist.

Stanley and Harriet saw a large statue of an Atlantean goddess near the Atlantean temples under the ocean in the ruins. They were very fascinated when they came near this enormous statue. Then they saw a dazzling, gold, religious statue of another goddess near the Atlantean temples.

Stanley and Harriet were absolutely enthralled when they personally encountered ancient, Atlantean ruins under the Atlantic Ocean in the Bahama Islands.

The Atlantean ruins were proof that an advanced, Atlantean civilization lived on Earth in this location.

Harriet and Stanley took a flight to Andros, another island in the Bahamas. They witnessed an enormous pyramid under the Atlantic Ocean. This was an Atlantean pyramid which sunk 100 feet under the Atlantic Ocean. Harriet and Stanley were astonished and surprised that an enormous, Atlantean pyramid existed in ancient Atlantis.

Harriet and Stanley flew home to Cleveland, Ohio refreshed, invigorated and renewed from their adventures in the Bahamian Islands. They had many, fascinating stories to tell their family and friends in the days and nights ahead.

FIFTY-SEVEN

SECRETARIES MAKE A DIFFERENCE

Secretaries are needed in every business. Businessmen and women need secretaries who can take accurate notes. Secretaries answer the phone to take messages. They file business papers and type business letters dictated by their bosses.

Secretaries do the paperwork for businesses. They have become the "right arm" for their bosses. Secretaries are able to look up specific information in files which are in A, B, C order. Specific letters can be taken out of the files to use regarding business issues and concerns.

Administrators and businessmen and women depend on their secretaries to do the paperwork to keep the business functioning. Secretaries record business matters and keep organized, pertinent information where it can be located in business offices.

Secretaries take shorthand and translate shorthand into English and other languages. Once shorthand notes are translated they are typed into letters, business reports and special memorandums. They are kept in alphabetical order and by specific, business accounts.

Without business records it would be difficult to do efficient business transactions. Written evidence is necessary to run an effective business. Secretaries are the backbone of any business.

Secretaries have many, important duties. Quite often they communicate with customers when the boss is away. They stand in for their boss when he is not present. A secretary is an important worker. Secretaries help maintain a daily routine in their offices in order to complete the necessary work.

So, if you can type, answer phone calls and you can write in shorthand and take good, accurate notes, you may qualify as a secretary. You may make a difference in the business world as a secretary.

FIFTY-EIGHT

INALIENABLE RIGHTS

We are all entitled to inalienable rights. We have the right to freedom of speech, freedom of religion, freedom to choose an occupation and freedom to communicate about issues, problems and different concepts. We have the right to vote so we can participate in choosing our political leaders. We are able to vote for new bills and propositions to improve our economy, environment, schools, healthcare programs and social welfare and security benefits.

Each inalienable right gives each person the right to live a better, freer life. Our American forefathers established equal, inalienable rights. Every person has the right to a good education, effective healthcare and a decent place to live.

Inalienable rights are God given rights. The integrity of every individual should be honored and protected. Every person should be treated equally and be treated fairly. Human rights are necessary to preserve liberty and freedom for all humanity.

FIFTY-NINE

COPING WITH CHANGES

Changes take place frequently. We should be willing to accept changes. We need to promote positive changes in order to improve our lives and the lives of others. We need to be flexible.

Effective leaders are able to make positive changes to help protect others. An effective leader is willing to develop policies, better laws and propositions. We must learn to cope with different changes.

If ineffective, political leaders are elected into office many people suffer from the consequences. Negative changes may take place. Ineffective, political leaders try to pass laws that take away our rights, or safety.

An ineffective leader signs bills that can harm many people.

There are many people who have to cope with poverty, diseases and poor, living conditions. Many uneducated people don't know much about political tricks. They may not know how to select the best political leaders. Ignorant, prejudiced individuals vote for the wrong propositions and bills which don't improve our economy, healthcare and banking methods, school programs and environmental issues and problems.

Positive changes are necessary so we can have a better way of life. We must select leaders who make wise decisions. Every wise decision makes a big difference in changing wrong conditions into right conditions.

Each of us needs to work for the good of all people. Each of us needs vision, insights and positive goals in order to accomplish what needs to be done to improve our world.

SIXTY

TRUTHFUL STATEMENTS

Each time we make truthful, honest statements we help ourselves ant others. George Washington made truthful statements. Abraham Lincoln made truthful statements. John F. Kennedy made truthful statements.

Jesus Christ made many truthful statements. He made a profound difference on Earth by setting an example for humanity. Honest, upright people who speak truthfully about many issues and problems can be trusted.

We should honor individuals who are honest and forthright. Honorable individuals do what is right and worthwhile. They make a real difference in the world. Every individual who speaks truthfully with conviction can help others.

Your truthful ideas and viewpoints will help you live a better, useful life. How you live your life will benefit yourself and others. Great leaders and individuals risk their lives for the sake of preserving the truth and freedom for themselves and others.